# EXERCISES IN ENGLISH

## ☆ GRAMMAR FOR LIFE ☆

## TEACHER'S EDITION

LEVEL F

LOYOLAPRESS.

CHICAGO

# The Complete Grammar Program with Character

*Enhancing Grammar with Grade-Level Science, Social Studies, Language Arts, and Character Education*

- **Instruction** and **practice** in every area of modern grammar, usage, and mechanics help students build comprehensive, lifelong skills.

- **Grade-level science, social studies,** and **language arts** content reinforces learning in other subject areas.

- **Character education** enriches students' lives through profiles of multicultural role models.

# A Six-Level Program

*Carefully sequenced Student Editions for grades 3–8 provide thorough teaching of all modern grammar concepts.*

*Easy-to-use Teacher's Editions offer clear, concise answers to exercises.*

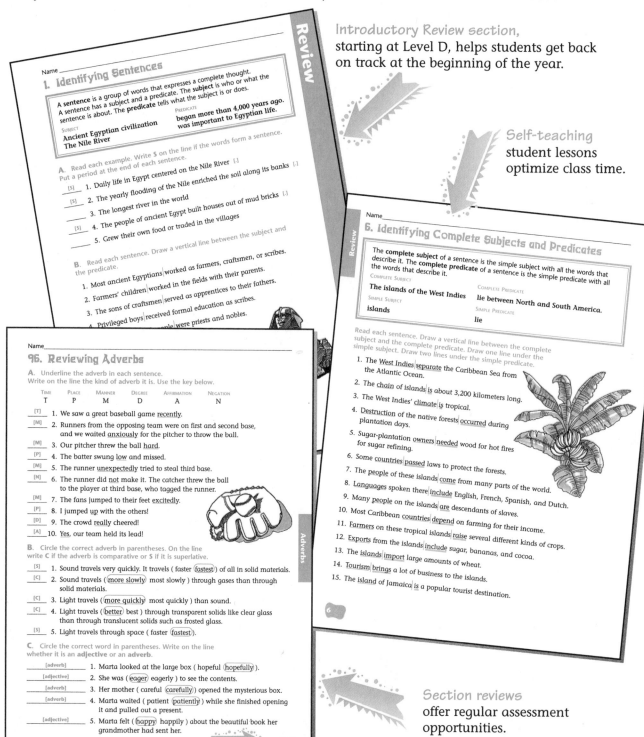

**Introductory Review section,** starting at Level D, helps students get back on track at the beginning of the year.

**Self-teaching** student lessons optimize class time.

**Section reviews** offer regular assessment opportunities.

---

Name_____

## 1. Identifying Sentences

A **sentence** is a group of words that expresses a complete thought. A sentence has a subject and a predicate. The **subject** is who or what the sentence is about. The **predicate** tells what the subject is or does.

SUBJECT
**Ancient Egyptian civilization**
**The Nile River**

PREDICATE
**began more than 4,000 years ago.**
**was important to Egyptian life.**

**A.** Read each example. Write **S** on the line if the words form a sentence. Put a period at the end of each sentence.

[S] 1. Daily life in Egypt centered on the Nile River [.]

[S] 2. The yearly flooding of the Nile enriched the soil along its banks [.]

3. The longest river in the world

[S] 4. The people of ancient Egypt built houses out of mud bricks [.]

5. Grew their own food or traded in the villages

**B.** Read each sentence. Draw a vertical line between the subject and the predicate.

1. Most ancient Egyptians|worked as farmers, craftsmen, or scribes.

2. Farmers' children|worked in the fields with their parents.

3. The sons of craftsmen|served as apprentices to their fathers.

4. Privileged boys|received formal education as scribes.

5. ...ple|were priests and nobles.

---

Name_____

## 6. Identifying Complete Subjects and Predicates

The **complete subject** of a sentence is the simple subject with all the words that describe it. The **complete predicate** of a sentence is the simple predicate with all the words that describe it.

COMPLETE SUBJECT
**The islands of the West Indies**

COMPLETE PREDICATE
**lie between North and South America.**

SIMPLE SUBJECT
**islands**

SIMPLE PREDICATE
**lie**

Read each sentence. Draw a vertical line between the complete subject and the complete predicate. Draw one line under the simple subject. Draw two lines under the simple predicate.

1. The West Indies|separate the Caribbean Sea from the Atlantic Ocean.

2. The chain of islands|is about 3,200 kilometers long.

3. The West Indies' climate|is tropical.

4. Destruction of the native forests|occurred during plantation days.

5. Sugar-plantation owners|needed wood for hot fires for sugar refining.

6. Some countries|passed laws to protect the forests.

7. The people of these islands|come from many parts of the world.

8. Languages spoken there|include English, French, Spanish, and Dutch.

9. Many people on the islands|are descendants of slaves.

10. Most Caribbean countries|depend on farming for their income.

11. Farmers on these tropical islands|raise several different kinds of crops.

12. Exports from the islands|include sugar, bananas, and cocoa.

13. The islands|import large amounts of wheat.

14. Tourism|brings a lot of business to the islands.

15. The island of Jamaica|is a popular tourist destination.

6

---

Name_____

## 96. Reviewing Adverbs

**A.** Underline the adverb in each sentence. Write on the line the kind of adverb it is. Use the key below.

| TIME | PLACE | MANNER | DEGREE | AFFIRMATION | NEGATION |
|------|-------|--------|--------|-------------|----------|
| T | P | M | D | A | N |

[T] 1. We saw a great baseball game <u>recently</u>.

[M] 2. Runners from the opposing team were on first and second base, and we waited <u>anxiously</u> for the pitcher to throw the ball.

[M] 3. Our pitcher threw the ball <u>hard</u>.

[P] 4. The batter swung <u>low</u> and missed.

[M] 5. The runner <u>unexpectedly</u> tried to steal third base.

[N] 6. The runner did <u>not</u> make it. The catcher threw the ball to the player at third base, who tagged the runner.

[M] 7. The fans jumped to their feet <u>excitedly</u>.

[P] 8. I jumped <u>up</u> with the others!

[D] 9. The crowd <u>really</u> cheered!

[A] 10. <u>Yes</u>, our team held its lead!

**B.** Circle the correct adverb in parentheses. On the line write **C** if the adverb is comparative or **S** if it is superlative.

[S] 1. Sound travels very quickly. It travels ( faster (fastest) ) of all in solid materials.

[C] 2. Sound travels ( (more slowly) most slowly ) through gases than through solid materials.

[C] 3. Light travels ( (more quickly) most quickly ) than sound.

[C] 4. Light travels ( (better) best ) through transparent solids like clear glass than through translucent solids such as frosted glass.

[S] 5. Light travels through space ( faster (fastest) ).

**C.** Circle the correct word in parentheses. Write on the line whether it is an **adjective** or an **adverb**.

[adverb] 1. Marta looked at the large box ( hopeful (hopefully) ).

[adjective] 2. She was ( (eager) eagerly ) to see the contents.

[adverb] 3. Her mother ( careful (carefully) ) opened the mysterious box.

[adverb] 4. Marta waited ( patient (patiently) ) while she finished opening it and pulled out a present.

[adjective] 5. Marta felt ( (happy) happily ) about the beautiful book her grandmother had sent her.

CONTINUED  101

---

# Features that set us apart...

## Clear definitions and examples
help students easily understand concepts.

---

### 14. Identifying Concrete and Abstract Nouns

A **concrete noun** names a thing that can be seen or touched.
**The Greek temple is at the top of a mountain.**

An **abstract noun** expresses a quality or a condition. It names something that cannot be seen or touched. Abstract nouns can be formed from other words by adding suffixes such as -dom, -hood, -ion, -tion, -ity, -ment, -ness, -ry, -ship, -th, and -ty.
**Democracy had its origin in ancient Greece.**

**A.** Underline the concrete nouns in each sentence. Circle the abstract nouns.

1. Sparta and Athens were two city states in ancient Greece.

---

**Verbs**

**A.** Underline the verb in each sentence. On the line write **T** if it is transitive, **I** if it is intransitive, or **L** if it is linking.

___[T]___ 1. People throughout the world eat salmon.

___[T]___ 2. Fishers catch millions of salmon each year.

___[L]___ 3. Salmon fishing remains an important industry.

___[I]___ 4. Many salmon live in the north part of the Pacific Ocean.

___[L]___ 5. The Atlantic salmon are native to the North Atlantic Ocean.

___[L]___ 6. Chinook are the largest species of salmon.

___[T]___ 7. Salmon lay their eggs in fresh water.

___[I]___ 8. The eggs hatch in fresh water.

___[I]___ 9. Some salmon travel up rivers during mating season.

___[L]___ 10. Salmon fishing is a popular sport on the Pacific coast.

**B.** Five of these sentences contain linking verbs. Underline the linking verb and circle the complement.

1. The salmon is famous for its long and difficult journeys.

2. At spawning time, salmon swim upstream.

3. They can leap over 10-foot waterfalls.

4. The male salmon is the protector of the female during spawning.

5. She deposits her eggs in a stream bed.

6. The male then fertilizes the eggs.

7. The eggs hatch after three or four months.

8. The young salmon are food for many predators.

9. The young salmon travel to the ocean and grow large.

10. Species of salmon sometimes become rare because of overfishing.

---

## Grade-level content
provides enrichment and reinforcement of what is being studied in science, social studies, and language arts.

---

### 17. Writing Plural Nouns

Complete each sentence with the plural form of the noun at the left.

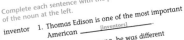

**Nouns**

inventor 1. Thomas Edison is one of the most important American ___[inventors]___.

child 2. When he was young, he was different from the other ___[children]___.

question 3. He was curious and was always asking ___[questions]___.

patent 4. During his career he held over 1,000 ___[patents]___ in his laboratory.

assistant 5. Edison had a team of ___[assistants]___.

supply 6. He set up a kind of "invention factory," in which he gave his workers materials and ___[supplies]___ needed for research.

discovery 7. Two of his most famous ___[discoveries]___ were the electric light bulb and the phonograph record.

movie 8. The film and projectors used to make and show ___[movies]___ were also his ideas.

camera 9. Of course, he had invented movie ___[cameras]___ too.

battery 10. He also developed a better way to make ___[batteries]___.

torpedo 11. During World War I, he helped the U.S. Army find ways to protect American ships from German ___[torpedoes]___.

engine 12. He also invented better forms of electrical ___[engines]___. His first engine is in a museum, and it still works!

factory 13. He designed and built ___[factories]___ to make chemicals, cement, and phonograph records.

key 14. One of the ___[keys]___ to Edison's success was reading: Before he began a project, he read a lot about the subject.

day 15. Three ___[days]___ after he died, much of America dimmed its lights for one minute in his honor.

Thomas Edison always read as much as he could before he started a new project. Give an example of a way you can use reading to help you.

---

## Character education lessons
offer students information on multicultural role models on a consistent basis.

---

about the group on the Web?

4. Isn't there ( nobody (anyone) ) ( (who) whom ) has observed animals in a natural setting?

5. Can't you tell us ( (anything) nothing ) about the person with ( who (whom) ) you have shared this experience?

**Try It Yourself**
Write four sentences about a person you admire. Tell what the person did or does. Explain why you admire him or her. Be sure to use pronouns correctly.

_____

_____

_____

_____

**Check Your Own Work**
Choose a selection from your writing portfolio, your journal, a work in progress, an assignment from another subject, or a letter. Revise it, applying the skills you have reviewed. The checklist will help you.

✔ Have you used subject and object pronouns correctly?

✔ Have you formed possessive pronouns correctly?

✔ Have you used interrogative pronouns in your sentences correctly?

✔ Have you avoided double negatives?

## Writing in context
allows students to practice and use what they have learned.

## 142. Using Guides to Periodicals

When you do research, you often need to find the latest information about a topic. Guides to periodical literature can be very helpful in finding such information. A **periodical** is anything published at regular intervals of more than one day. Magazines are periodicals; daily newspapers are not.

One helpful guide is the *Children's Magazine Guide*. Articles from about 50 periodicals are indexed in the *Children's Magazine Guide*. It is published monthly from August through March and semimonthly for April and May. August is a yearlong cumulative issue.

All entries are listed in alphabetical order by subject. The *Guide* includes listings for scientific articles, articles about computers, art topics, movie reviews, poetry, and so on. Many subjects are cross-referenced to other subject headings.

Look at the sample entry below, including the labels.

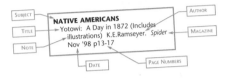

The *Reader's Guide to Periodical Literature* is another index of periodicals. It is published semimonthly and also can be found online in some libraries. In it you can check for information by author or by subject. When you use it, you may need to ask a librarian to help you understand some of the abbreviations.

Research Skills section provides teaching and practice with tools such as the Internet and atlases. Students learn to combine grammar and writing in projects for other classes.

Handbook of Terms helps students refresh and expand their knowledge of grammar points.

Conjunctions connect independent clauses: It poured all day, and a cold wind blew. An independent clause has a subject and a predicate and expresses a complete thought.

**contraction** Two words written as one with one or more letters omitted: *doesn't* for *does not, I've* for *I have.*

An apostrophe is used to show the omission of a letter or letters. Subject pronouns are used with verbs to form contractions: *we're* for *we are, she's* for *she is.*

**D**

**dash** A punctuation mark (—) used to indicate a sudden change of thought: The boy jumped—indeed soared—over the hurdle.

**direct object** The receiver of the action of a verb: Nathaniel gave the *baby* to his mother.

An object pronoun can be used as a direct object: Nathaniel gave *him* to his mother.

**E**

**exclamation point** A punctuation mark (!) used after an exclamatory sentence and after an exclamatory word or phrase: More than one thousand people attended the wedding! Wonderful! What a celebration!

**H**

**hyphen** A punctuation mark (-) used to divide a word at the end of a line whenever one or more syllables are carried to the next line.

The hyphen is also used in the words for compound numbers from twenty-one to ninety-nine and to separate the parts of some compound words: *soldier-statesman, half-baked* plan.

**I**

**indefinite pronoun** An indefinite pronoun refers to any or all of a group of persons, places, or things or separately to each member of a group of persons, places, or things. Indefinite pronouns include: *each, either, neither, anyone, no one, anybody, nobody, everyone, everybody, someone, somebody, nothing, something, both, few, many, several, all,* and *some:* Almost *everyone* had a second helping of the pie.

Sentence Diagramming section, starting at Level D, helps students visually portray the parts of a sentence to better understand and remember concepts.

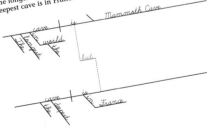

**D.** This simple sentence has a compound predicate. Indicate a compound predicate the same way as a compound subject. Add object, complements, and modifiers to the appropriate words.

The old gardener raked the fallen leaves and mowed the long grass.

### Diagramming a Compound Sentence

A compound sentence contains two or more independent clauses. Each clause is diagrammed according to the form for a simple sentence. When both independent clauses have been diagrammed, place the conjunction on a horizontal line between the verbs and connect it to the main diagram lines with broken vertical lines.

The longest cave in the world is Mammoth Cave, but the deepest cave is in France.

## Plus

- **Flexible format** allows use of the books at multiple grade levels.

- **Perforated student pages** facilitate grading and inclusion in student portfolios.

- **Easy-to-grade exercises** are always divisible by five.

- **Sentence Analysis section** in the Teacher's Edition provides extra tools for daily oral grammar activities.

# Exercises in English—Scope and Sequence

| SENTENCES | C | D | E | F | G | H |
|---|---|---|---|---|---|---|
| The Four Kinds of Sentences | ✔ | ✔ | ✔ | ✔ | ✔ | ✔ |
| Subjects and Predicates | ✔ | ✔ | ✔ | ✔ | ✔ | ✔ |
| Simple Subjects and Predicates | | ✔ | | ✔ | ✔ | ✔ |
| Compound Subjects and Predicates | | ✔ | ✔ | ✔ | ✔ | ✔ |
| Direct Objects | | ✔ | ✔ | ✔ | ✔ | ✔ |
| Complete Subjects and Predicates | | | ✔ | ✔ | ✔ | ✔ |
| Natural and Inverted Order in Sentences | | | ✔ | ✔ | ✔ | ✔ |
| Indirect Objects | | | | ✔ | ✔ | ✔ |
| Compound Sentences | | | | ✔ | ✔ | ✔ |
| Complex Sentences | | | | | ✔ | ✔ |
| Compound Complex Sentences | | | | | | ✔ |
| **NOUNS** | C | D | E | F | G | H |
| Proper and Common Nouns | ✔ | ✔ | ✔ | ✔ | ✔ | ✔ |
| Singular and Plural Nouns | ✔ | ✔ | ✔ | ✔ | ✔ | ✔ |
| Possessive Nouns | ✔ | ✔ | ✔ | ✔ | ✔ | ✔ |
| Nouns Used as Subjects | | ✔ | ✔ | ✔ | | |
| Nouns Used as Objects | | ✔ | ✔ | ✔ | ✔ | ✔ |
| Nouns Used as Subject Complements | | | ✔ | ✔ | ✔ | |
| Nouns Used in Direct Address | | | ✔ | ✔ | | |
| Nouns Used as Objects of Prepositions | | | ✔ | ✔ | ✔ | |
| Appositives | | | | ✔ | ✔ | |
| Collective Nouns | | | | ✔ | ✔ | ✔ |
| Concrete and Abstract Nouns | | | | ✔ | ✔ | ✔ |
| Words Used as Nouns and Verbs | | | | ✔ | | ✔ |
| Nouns Used as Object Complements | | | | | | ✔ |
| **VERBS** | C | D | E | F | G | H |
| Regular and Irregular Verbs | ✔ | ✔ | ✔ | ✔ | ✔ | ✔ |
| Present Tense | ✔ | ✔ | ✔ | ✔ | ✔ | ✔ |
| Progressive Tenses | ✔ | ✔ | ✔ | ✔ | ✔ | ✔ |
| Past Tense | ✔ | ✔ | ✔ | ✔ | ✔ | ✔ |
| Future Tenses | ✔ | ✔ | ✔ | ✔ | ✔ | ✔ |
| Action Verbs | ✔ | ✔ | ✔ | | | |
| Verbs of Being | ✔ | ✔ | ✔ | | | |
| Helping Verbs | ✔ | ✔ | | | | |
| Forms of *Bring* | ✔ | | | | | |
| Forms of *Buy* | ✔ | | | | | |

| | | | | | | |
|---|---|---|---|---|---|---|
| Forms of *Come* | ✔ | | | | | |
| Forms of *Eat* | ✔ | | | | | |
| Forms of *Go* | ✔ | | ✔ | | | |
| Forms of *See* | ✔ | | ✔ | | | |
| Forms of *Sit* and *Set* | ✔ | | ✔ | ✔ | | |
| Forms of *Take* | ✔ | | ✔ | | | |
| Forms of *Write* | ✔ | | | | | |
| Forms of *To Be* | ✔ | ✔ | ✔ | | | |
| Forms of *Begin* | | ✔ | | | | |
| Forms of *Break* | | ✔ | ✔ | | | |
| Forms of *Choose* | | ✔ | ✔ | | | |
| Forms of *Do* | | ✔ | | | | |
| Verb Phrases | | ✔ | ✔ | ✔ | ✔ | |
| Intransitive Verbs (Linking Verbs) | | ✔ | ✔ | ✔ | ✔ | ✔ |
| *There Is* and *There Are* | | ✔ | | ✔ | ✔ | |
| Subject-Verb Agreement | | | ✔ | ✔ | ✔ | ✔ |
| Transitive Verbs | | | ✔ | ✔ | ✔ | ✔ |
| *Doesn't* and *Don't* | | | ✔ | ✔ | ✔ | ✔ |
| *Let* and *Leave* | | | ✔ | ✔ | | |
| *Teach* and *Learn* | | | ✔ | | | |
| *Lie* and *Lay* | | | ✔ | ✔ | | |
| *Rise* and *Raise* | | | | ✔ | | |
| Perfect Tenses | | | | ✔ | ✔ | |
| Words Used as Nouns and Verbs | | | | | ✔ | |
| Active and Passive Voice | | | | | ✔ | ✔ |
| Modal Auxiliary Verbs | | | | | ✔ | ✔ |
| *You Are* and *You Were* | | | | | ✔ | |
| Compound Tenses | | | | | | ✔ |
| Emphatic Verb Forms | | | | | | ✔ |
| **PRONOUNS** | C | D | E | F | G | H |
| Singular and Plural Pronouns | ✔ | ✔ | ✔ | | | |
| Subject Pronouns | ✔ | ✔ | ✔ | ✔ | ✔ | ✔ |
| Possessive Pronouns | ✔ | ✔ | ✔ | ✔ | ✔ | ✔ |
| *I* and *Me* | ✔ | ✔ | | | | |
| Pronouns Used as Subject Complements | ✔ | | ✔ | ✔ | ✔ | ✔ |
| Pronouns Used as Direct Objects | | ✔ | ✔ | ✔ | ✔ | ✔ |
| The Person of Pronouns | | ✔ | ✔ | ✔ | | |
| The Gender of Pronouns | | | ✔ | | | |
| *We* and *Us* | | ✔ | | | | |
| Pronouns Used as Objects of Prepositions | | | ✔ | ✔ | | |

| | C | D | E | F | G | H |
|---|---|---|---|---|---|---|
| Pronouns Used in Contractions | | | ✔ | ✔ | | |
| Reflexive Pronouns | | | ✔ | ✔ | ✔ | |
| Interrogative Pronouns | | | | ✔ | ✔ | ✔ |
| Indefinite Pronouns | | | | ✔ | ✔ | ✔ |
| Double Negatives | | | | ✔ | | |
| Pronouns Used as Indirect Objects | | | | | ✔ | ✔ |
| Who and Whom | | | | | ✔ | ✔ |
| Pronouns Used after Than and As | | | | | ✔ | ✔ |
| Relative Pronouns | | | | | ✔ | ✔ |
| Demonstrative Pronouns | | | | | ✔ | ✔ |
| Nothing and Anything | | | | | ✔ | |
| Pronouns Used as Objects of Prepositions | | | | | | ✔ |
| Intensive Pronouns | | | ✔ | | | ✔ |
| **ADJECTIVES** | **C** | **D** | **E** | **F** | **G** | **H** |
| Descriptive Adjectives | ✔ | | | ✔ | ✔ | |
| Adjectives That Tell How Many | ✔ | ✔ | ✔ | ✔ | | |
| Indefinite and Definite Articles | ✔ | ✔ | ✔ | ✔ | ✔ | |
| Demonstrative Adjectives | ✔ | ✔ | ✔ | ✔ | ✔ | ✔ |
| Comparative Forms of Adjectives | ✔ | ✔ | ✔ | ✔ | ✔ | ✔ |
| Possessive Adjectives | | ✔ | ✔ | ✔ | | |
| Common and Proper Adjectives | | ✔ | ✔ | | | ✔ |
| Good and Bad | | ✔ | | | | |
| The Position of Adjectives | | | ✔ | ✔ | ✔ | ✔ |
| Superlative Forms of Adjectives | | | ✔ | ✔ | ✔ | ✔ |
| Adjectives Used as Subject Complements | | | | ✔ | | |
| Words Used as Adjectives or Nouns | | | | ✔ | ✔ | ✔ |
| Those and Them | | | | ✔ | | |
| Interrogative Adjectives | | | | ✔ | | |
| Fewer and Less | | | | | ✔ | |
| **ADVERBS** | **C** | **D** | **E** | **F** | **G** | **H** |
| Adverbs of Time | ✔ | ✔ | ✔ | ✔ | | |
| Adverbs of Place | ✔ | ✔ | ✔ | ✔ | | |
| Good and Well | ✔ | ✔ | ✔ | | | |
| Comparative Adverbs | | ✔ | ✔ | ✔ | ✔ | ✔ |
| Adverbs of Manner | | ✔ | ✔ | ✔ | | |
| No, Not, and Never | | ✔ | ✔ | ✔ | | |
| Superlative Adverbs | | | ✔ | ✔ | | |
| Real and Very | | | ✔ | | | |
| Their and There | | | ✔ | ✔ | | |
| To, Too, and Two | | | ✔ | ✔ | | |

| | C | D | E | F | G | H |
|---|---|---|---|---|---|---|
| Adverbs and Adjectives | | | | ✔ | ✔ | ✔ |
| *There, Their,* and *They're* | | | | | ✔ | |
| *Farther* and *Further* | | | | | ✔ | ✔ |
| Interrogative Adverbs | | | | | ✔ | ✔ |
| Adverbial Nouns | | | | | ✔ | ✔ |
| *As . . . As, So . . . As,* and *Equally* | | | | | | ✔ |

| PUNCTUATION, CAPITALIZATION, ABBREVIATIONS | C | D | E | F | G | H |
|---|---|---|---|---|---|---|
| End Punctuation | ✔ | ✔ | ✔ | ✔ | ✔ | ✔ |
| Periods after Abbreviations, Titles, and Initials | ✔ | ✔ | | | | |
| Capital Letters | ✔ | ✔ | ✔ | ✔ | ✔ | |
| Titles of Books and Poems | ✔ | | ✔ | ✔ | ✔ | |
| Commas Used in Direct Address | ✔ | ✔ | ✔ | ✔ | | |
| Punctuation in Direct Quotations | ✔ | ✔ | ✔ | ✔ | | |
| Apostrophes | | ✔ | ✔ | | | |
| Commas after *Yes* and *No* | | ✔ | ✔ | ✔ | | |
| Commas Separating Words in a Series | | ✔ | ✔ | ✔ | | |
| Commas after Parts of a Letter | | | ✔ | ✔ | | |
| Commas in Dates and Addresses | | | ✔ | ✔ | | |
| Commas in Geographical Names | | | ✔ | | | |
| Commas Used with Appositives | | | | ✔ | | |
| Commas Used in Compound Sentences | | | | ✔ | | |
| Semicolons and Colons | | | | ✔ | ✔ | ✔ |
| Apostrophes, Hyphens, and Dashes | | | | ✔ | ✔ | ✔ |
| Commas and Semicolons | | | | | | ✔ |

| PREPOSITIONS, CONJUNCTIONS, INTERJECTIONS | C | D | E | F | G | H |
|---|---|---|---|---|---|---|
| Prepositions and Prepositional Phrases | | | ✔ | ✔ | ✔ | ✔ |
| Interjections | | | ✔ | ✔ | ✔ | ✔ |
| *Between* and *Among* | | | ✔ | ✔ | | |
| *From* and *Off* | | | ✔ | | | |
| Adjectival Phrases | | | ✔ | | | |
| Adverbial Phrases | | | ✔ | | | |
| Coordinate Conjunctions | | | ✔ | | | |
| Words Used as Prepositions and Adverbs | | | | ✔ | ✔ | ✔ |
| *At* and *To* | | | | ✔ | | |
| *Beside* and *Besides, In* and *Into* | | | | ✔ | | |
| Coordinate and Correlative Conjunctions | | | | | ✔ | |
| Conjunctive Adverbs | | | | | ✔ | |

| | C | D | E | F | G | H |
|---|---|---|---|---|---|---|
| Subordinate Conjunctions | | | | | ✔ | ✔ |
| *Without* and *Unless, Like, As,* and *As If* | | | | | ✔ | ✔ |
| **PHRASES, CLAUSES** | C | D | E | F | G | H |
| Adjectival Phrases | | | | ✔ | ✔ | |
| Adverbial Phrases | | | | ✔ | ✔ | |
| Adjectival Clauses | | | | | ✔ | ✔ |
| Adverbial Clauses | | | | | ✔ | ✔ |
| Restrictive and Nonrestrictive Clauses | | | | | ✔ | |
| Noun Clauses | | | | | | ✔ |
| **PARTICIPLES, GERUNDS, INFINITIVES** | C | D | E | F | G | H |
| Participles | | | | | | ✔ |
| Dangling Participles | | | | | | ✔ |
| Gerunds | | | | | | ✔ |
| Infinitives | | | | | | ✔ |
| Hidden and Split Infinitives | | | | | | ✔ |
| **WORD STUDY SKILLS** | C | D | E | F | G | H |
| Synonyms | ✔ | ✔ | ✔ | ✔ | | |
| Antonyms | ✔ | ✔ | | | | |
| Homophones | ✔ | ✔ | ✔ | | | |
| Contractions | ✔ | ✔ | | | | |
| Compound Words | | ✔ | | | | |
| **PARAGRAPH SKILLS** | C | D | E | F | G | H |
| Using Colorful Adjectives | ✔ | | ✔ | | | |
| Combining Subjects, Verbs, and Sentences | ✔ | | | | | |
| Finding the Exact Word | | ✔ | | | | |
| Using Similes | | ✔ | | | | |
| Expanding Sentences | | ✔ | | | | |
| Rewriting Rambling Sentences | | ✔ | ✔ | | | |
| Revising | | ✔ | | | | |
| Proofreading | | ✔ | | | | |
| Recognizing the Exact Meaning of Words | | | ✔ | | | |
| **LETTER WRITING** | C | D | E | F | G | H |
| Friendly Letters | ✔ | ✔ | | | | |
| Invitations | ✔ | | | | | |
| Letters of Acceptance | ✔ | | | | | |
| Thank-You Letters | ✔ | | | ✔ | | |
| E-Mail Messages | ✔ | ✔ | | ✔ | | |

| | C | D | E | F | G | H |
|---|---|---|---|---|---|---|
| Envelopes | ✔ | ✔ | | | | |
| Forms | ✔ | ✔ | | | | |
| Business Letters | | | | ✔ | | |
| **RESEARCH** | C | D | E | F | G | H |
| Computer Catalog | ✔ | | | | | |
| Dictionary | ✔ | ✔ | | | | |
| Encyclopedia | ✔ | | ✔ | | | |
| Thesaurus | | ✔ | | | | |
| Internet | | ✔ | ✔ | ✔ | ✔ | ✔ |
| Almanac | | | ✔ | | | |
| Atlas | | | ✔ | | ✔ | |
| Guides to Periodicals | | | | ✔ | | |
| Biographical Information | | | | ✔ | | |
| The Dewey Decimal System | | | | ✔ | | |
| Books of Quotations | | | | | ✔ | |
| Books in Print | | | | | ✔ | |
| The Statistical Abstract of the United States | | | | | | ✔ |
| Research Tools | | | | | | ✔ |

# Sentence Analysis

## Purpose

Sentence analysis is a classroom-tested strategy designed to aid students in the understanding of a sentence through the study of its grammatical components and their relationship to one another.

Sentence analysis begins with a careful and thoughtful reading of the sentence to determine that it does contain a complete thought. Students then determine the *use* of the sentence (for example, declarative). Next, they identify the subject and the predicate. They can then go on to analyze the details in the sentence.

It is often useful to conduct a sentence analysis as an oral exercise. Each student responds to one point in the analysis in some predetermined order—by row, by group, or by number. Keep the responses moving at a fairly fast pace to hold students' interest. Five minutes at the beginning of each grammar period will focus the students on the task. Prolonging the activity may make it a chore rather than a challenge.

Give each student a copy of the Sentence Analysis Chart (page TE16) or place a blown-up version where all students can see it. Select a sentence from this or another book and write it on the board for analysis.

Ideally, you should act as an observer during the activity, allowing students to perform the analysis without assistance. The students' performance will indicate their grasp of grammar and help you identify areas that need review.

Consistent practice in identifying grammatical concepts will ensure that students arrive at an understanding of how the English language is structured and how they can use its patterns to express their own thoughts.

## Procedure

Display the Sentence Analysis Chart (page TE16) or distribute a copy to each student. Choose a sentence that contains the aspects of grammar recently taught or reviewed and write it on the board. The first few times you do the activity, you may also want to display or distribute the Sentence Analysis Questions (page TE15) to help students complete the task.

Now have students use the chart to work through the steps of analysis, identifying each part of the sentence.

### 1. Sentence

Have the sentence read aloud. You may want to have the class read as a whole or ask an individual to read. Students should recognize that a sentence has a subject and a predicate and forms a complete thought.

EXAMPLE SENTENCE: **Yesterday the happy children played drums noisily.**

## 2. Use

Students should be able to recognize that a sentence is declarative, interrogative, imperative, or exclamatory. In selecting sentences for analysis, vary your choice among the four types.

According to *use*, the example sentence is declarative because it makes a statement.

**Note:** You may want to have students practice steps 1 and 2 several times before moving on to step 3. Once the students are comfortable identifying sentences, add the following steps one at a time, practicing them in short sessions each day.

## 3. Predicate

The predicate is the part of a sentence that contains a verb. Because the verb is the focal point of the thought, it should be identified first. The verb expresses action or being.

The verb in the example sentence is *played.*

## 4. Subject

The verb tells what the subject does or is. The subject can be determined by asking *who* or *what* before the verb.

The subject of the example sentence is *children.*

## 5. Object/Complement

Sometimes the predicate verb is completed by a direct object or a subject complement. They answer the questions *whom, who,* or *what* after the verb.

The direct object of the example sentece is *drums.*

## 6. Modifiers

Adverbs modify verbs. Adverbs answer the questions *how, when,* or *where.*

In the example sentence, the adverb *yesterday* tells when the children played, and the adverb *noisily* tells how the children played.

Adjectives modify nouns or pronouns. Adjectives answer the questions *what, what kind, how many,* or *whose.* An article is an adjective that points out a noun.

In the example sentence, the article *the* points out the noun *children,* and the adjective *happy* tells what kind of children.

## 7. Parts of Speech

To close the activity, ask the students to name the part of speech of each word in the sentence, beginning with the first and moving through the sentence in order.

In the example sentence, *yesterday* is an adverb, *the* is an article, *happy* is an adjective, *children* is a noun, *played* is a verb, *noisily* is an adverb.

# Sentence Analysis Questions

## 1. Sentence
Does the group of words form a complete thought with a subject and a predicate? (If it does, it's a sentence.)

## 2. Use
Is the sentence *declarative* (makes a statement), *interrogative* (asks a question), *imperative* (gives a command), or *exclamatory* (shows surprise or emotion)?

## 3. Predicate
The predicate of a sentence contains a *verb*. A verb shows action or being. What is the verb in the sentence? (The verb includes the main verb and any helping verbs: *swam/had swum, goes/is going.*)

## 4. Subject
The *subject* is a noun or a pronoun. The verb tells what the subject does or is. To find the subject, ask *who* or *what* before the verb.

## 5. Object/Complement
The direct object or subject complement complete the verb. To find them ask *whom, who,* or *what* after the verb.

## 6. Modifiers
Adverbs tell more about verbs. To find the adverbs, ask *how, when,* or *where* the action or being took place.

Adjectives describe nouns or pronouns. To find the adjectives, ask *what, what kind, how many,* or *whose* about each noun or pronoun. An article is an adjective that points out a noun.

## 7. Parts of Speech
- Which words name persons, places, or things? (Those words are *nouns.*)
- Which words take the place of nouns? (Those words are *pronouns.*)
- Which words express action or being? (Those words are *verbs.*)
- Which words tell more about verbs? (Those words are *adverbs.*)
- Which words describe nouns? (Those words are *adjectives.*)

# Sentence Analysis Chart

Sentence

Use

Predicate

Subject

Object/Complement

Modifiers

Parts of Speech

# EXERCISES IN ENGLISH

## ☆ GRAMMAR FOR LIFE ☆

### LEVEL F

LOYOLAPRESS.

CHICAGO

## Consultants
Therese Elizabeth Bauer
Martina Anne Erdlen
Anita Patrick Gallagher
Patricia Healey
Irene Kervick
Susan Platt

## Linguistics Advisor
Timothy G. Collins
National-Louis University

**Series Design:** Karen Christoffersen
**Cover Design:** Vita Jay Schweighart
**Cover Art:** Jody Lepinot/prairiestudio.com
**Cover Photoshop:** Becca Taylor Gay
**Interior Art:** Mona Mark/Represented by Anita Grien
**Character Education Portraits:** Jim Mitchell
**Back Cover Text:** Ted Naron

## Acknowledgments

| | |
|---|---|
| page 154 | Excerpt from *Children's Magazine Guide* reprinted with the permission of R. R. Bowker, a division of Reed Elseveier Inc. Copyright 1999, Reed Elsevier Inc. |
| page 155 | Biography of Amelia Earhart reprinted by permission of Eric Tentarelli, S9.com. |

0-8294-2019-3 ★

0-8294-1748-6 ★

Exercises in English® is a registered trademark of Loyola Press.

# Table of Contents

Name _____

# 1. Identifying Sentences

A **sentence** is a group of words that expresses a complete thought.
A sentence has a subject and a predicate. The **subject** is who or what the
sentence is about. The **predicate** tells what the subject is or does.

SUBJECT
Ancient Egyptian civilization
The Nile River

PREDICATE
began more than 4,000 years ago.
was important to Egyptian life.

**A.** Read each example. Write **S** on the line if the words form a sentence.
Put a period at the end of each sentence.

___[S]___ 1. Daily life in Egypt centered on the Nile River [.]

___[S]___ 2. The yearly flooding of the Nile enriched the soil along its banks [.]

_____ 3. The longest river in the world

___[S]___ 4. The people of ancient Egypt built houses out of mud bricks [.]

_____ 5. Grew their own food or traded in the villages

**B.** Read each sentence. Draw a vertical line between the subject and
the predicate.

1. Most ancient Egyptians│worked as farmers, craftsmen, or scribes.

2. Farmers' children│worked in the fields with their parents.

3. The sons of craftsmen│served as apprentices to their fathers.

4. Privileged boys│received formal education as scribes.

5. A small group of people│were priests and nobles.

6. The pharaoh│dominated ancient
   Egyptian government.

7. The people of Egypt│considered him a god.

8. The pharaoh's advisors│were the priests.

9. Both men and women in
   ancient Egypt│wore cosmetics.

10. Oils and creams│protected people's skin
    from the sun and wind.

**Review**

# 2. Identifying Declarative and Interrogative Sentences

A **declarative sentence** makes a statement.
A declarative sentence ends with a period.

**A volcano is an opening in the earth's crust.**

An **interrogative sentence** asks a question.
An interrogative sentence ends with a question mark.

**Why do volcanoes erupt?**

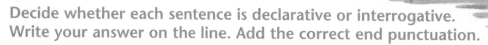

Decide whether each sentence is declarative or interrogative.
Write your answer on the line. Add the correct end punctuation.

_____[declarative]_____ 1. Volcanoes have magma chambers inside them [.]

_____[interrogative]_____ 2. What is magma [?]

_____[declarative]_____ 3. Magma is molten rock [.]

_____[declarative]_____ 4. Volcanoes erupt because of density and pressure [.]

_____[interrogative]_____ 5. How does density affect a volcano [?]

_____[declarative]_____ 6. Magma is less dense than the surrounding rocks are [.]

_____[declarative]_____ 7. Bubbles of gas form in the magma [.]

_____[interrogative]_____ 8. What happens when the bubbles rise [?]

_____[declarative]_____ 9. The bubbles exert tremendous pressure on the rock [.]

_____[declarative]_____ 10. The pressure pushes the magma and rock out of the earth [.]

_____[interrogative]_____ 11. Is there molten rock on the surface of the earth [?]

_____[declarative]_____ 12. Lava is molten rock [.]

_____[declarative]_____ 13. In some volcanoes lava oozes out slowly [.]

_____[interrogative]_____ 14. Do some volcanoes explode violently [?]

_____[declarative]_____ 15. Rock, ash, and cinders can shoot out of openings [.]

_____[interrogative]_____ 16. How often do volcanoes erupt [?]

_____[declarative]_____ 17. Some volcanoes erupt more often than others [.]

_____[declarative]_____ 18. On average Kilauea in Hawaii erupts every 3.95 years [.]

_____[declarative]_____ 19. Mount St. Helens erupted in 1980 [.]

_____[declarative]_____ 20. It hadn't erupted in more than 120 years [.]

# 3. Identifying Imperative and Exclamatory Sentences

> An **imperative sentence** gives a command or makes a request.
> An imperative sentence ends with a period.
>
> **Explain the nature of friction.**
>
> An **exclamatory sentence** expresses a strong emotion.
> An exclamatory sentence ends with an exclamation mark.
>
> **That's truly amazing!**

**A.** Underline the sentences that are imperative.

1. Friction makes moving in water difficult.

2. Take a smooth rubber ball and a tennis ball.

3. Put a little water into a shallow bowl.

4. Try spinning each ball in the bowl.

5. Which one spins more easily?

6. Write your results in your journal.

7. The rubber ball is smoother than the tennis ball.

8. The smooth surface causes less friction.

9. That's why a fast boat has a smooth hull.

10. Think of another experiment to do with friction.

**B.** Decide whether each sentence is imperative or exclamatory.
Write your answer on the line. Add the correct end punctuation.

_____[imperative]_____ 1. Get a glass jar with a lid [.]

_____[imperative]_____ 2. Have some soap and water ready [.]

_____[imperative]_____ 3. Screw the cover on the jar as tightly as you can [.]

_____[exclamatory]_____ 4. Be careful [!]

_____[exclamatory]_____ 5. Wow, that's really tight [!]

_____[imperative]_____ 6. Wet your hands with the soap and water [.]

_____[imperative]_____ 7. Try to take the lid off the jar [.]

_____[exclamatory]_____ 8. It's impossible [!]

_____[imperative]_____ 9. Make an observation about friction [.]

_____[exclamatory]_____ 10. Think really hard [!]

Review

# 4. Identifying the Four Kinds of Sentences

A sentence can be declarative, interrogative, imperative, or exclamatory.

Decide whether each sentence is declarative, interrogative, imperative, or exclamatory. Write your answer on the line. Add the correct end punctuation.

_____[declarative]_____ 1. Irving Berlin was one of America's most successful songwriters [.]

_____[interrogative]_____ 2. Do you know the names of any of his songs [?]

_____[declarative]_____ 3. "White Christmas" and "God Bless America" are among his songs [.]

_____[declarative]_____ 4. Berlin couldn't read or write music or play the piano very well [.]

_____[exclamatory]_____ 5. That's incredible [!]

_____[declarative]_____ 6. During World War II Berlin wrote a musical about the army [.]

_____[imperative]_____ 7. Name the dates for World War II [.]

_____[declarative]_____ 8. The show raised $10,000,000 for charity [.]

_____[exclamatory]_____ 9. That's what I call impressive [!]

_____[declarative]_____ 10. Berlin was born in Russia in 1888 [.]

_____[interrogative]_____ 11. Why did the family move to the United States [?]

_____[declarative]_____ 12. There was discrimination against Jews in Russia [.]

_____[declarative]_____ 13. Berlin wrote many patriotic songs about America [.]

_____[interrogative]_____ 14. Can you sing one of his songs [?]

_____[imperative]_____ 15. Try to find out more about Irving Berlin [.]

Irving Berlin believed that music could cheer people up and give them courage. Give an example of how you can cheer people up and give them courage.

Name_____

# 5. Identifying Simple Subjects and Predicates

A sentence has a subject and a predicate. The **simple subject** is the noun or pronoun that names the person, place, or thing the sentence is about. The **simple predicate** is the verb that tells what the subject does or is.

| SIMPLE SUBJECT | SIMPLE PREDICATE |
|---|---|
| Water | evaporates. |
| Cold water | evaporates slowly. |
| Water at the boiling point | evaporates very quickly. |

**A.** Write the simple subject and simple predicate of each sentence in the correct column.

|  | SIMPLE SUBJECT | SIMPLE PREDICATE |
|---|---|---|
| 1. Plants need water. | [Plants] | [need] |
| 2. Plants in the desert get water in many ways. | [Plants] | [get] |
| 3. A cactus stores water in its thick stem. | [cactus] | [stores] |
| 4. Some plants have very long roots. | [plants] | [have] |
| 5. These long roots reach water deep underground. | [roots] | [reach] |
| 6. Flowers bloom after a rainstorm. | [Flowers] | [bloom] |
| 7. Animals need water too. | [Animals] | [need] |
| 8. Many animals in the desert rest all day. | [animals] | [rest] |
| 9. Foxes hunt in the cool evenings. | [Foxes] | [hunt] |
| 10. Their food provides some animals with water. | [food] | [provides] |

**B.** Read each sentence. Draw one line under the simple subject. Draw two lines under the simple predicate.

1. Animals in the ocean obtain air and food from the water around them.

2. Some ocean animals hunt for food.

3. Other kinds always stay in one place.

4. Microscopic animals in the water are an important source of food.

5. Whales filter animals from seawater for food.

Review

5

# 6. Identifying Complete Subjects and Predicates

> The **complete subject** of a sentence is the simple subject with all the words that describe it. The **complete predicate** of a sentence is the simple predicate with all the words that describe it.
>
> COMPLETE SUBJECT
> **The islands of the West Indies**
>
> COMPLETE PREDICATE
> **lie between North and South America.**
>
> SIMPLE SUBJECT
> **islands**
>
> SIMPLE PREDICATE
> **lie**

Read each sentence. Draw a vertical line between the complete subject and the complete predicate. Draw one line under the simple subject. Draw two lines under the simple predicate.

1. The West Indies | separate the Caribbean Sea from the Atlantic Ocean.

2. The chain of islands | is about 3,200 kilometers long.

3. The West Indies' climate | is tropical.

4. Destruction of the native forests | occurred during plantation days.

5. Sugar-plantation owners | needed wood for hot fires for sugar refining.

6. Some countries | passed laws to protect the forests.

7. The people of these islands | come from many parts of the world.

8. Languages spoken there | include English, French, Spanish, and Dutch.

9. Many people on the islands | are descendants of slaves.

10. Most Caribbean countries | depend on farming for their income.

11. Farmers on these tropical islands | raise several different kinds of crops.

12. Exports from the islands | include sugar, bananas, and cocoa.

13. The islands | import large amounts of wheat.

14. Tourism | brings a lot of business to the islands.

15. The island of Jamaica | is a popular tourist destination.

Name_____

# 7. Forming Sentences

| A sentence has a subject and a predicate. |
| --- |

**A.** Make sentences by matching the complete subjects in the
first column with the complete predicates in the second column.
Write the correct letter on the line. Use each letter once.

_[d]_ 1. For nourishment grizzly bears     a. can weigh up to 600 pounds.

_[h]_ 2. Brown bear     b. lasts for 5 to 6 months through
   the winter.

_[f]_ 3. A grizzly's fur     c. frighten people.

_[i]_ 4. A grizzly's diet     d. eat both plants and animals.

_[c]_ 5. The grizzly's claws     e. is one of the grizzly's food sources.

_[g]_ 6. Dens high in the mountains     f. can range from white to blonde
   to pure black.

_[b]_ 7. Grizzly bear hibernation     g. are where grizzlies hibernate.

_[j]_ 8. Mother grizzlies     h. is what a grizzly is called in Alaska.

_[a]_ 9. A fully grown male grizzly     i. can consist of fruits and berries.

_[e]_ 10. Salmon     j. are very protective of their cubs.

**B.** Choose the best simple predicate to complete each sentence.
Use each word or phrase once.

   **cover**     **have existed**     **house**     **remains**     **receives**

1. Rain forests _____[cover]_____ 6 percent of
   the earth's land surface.

2. They _____[house]_____ more than half of
   all plant and animal species on earth.

3. A rain forest _____[receives]_____ from
   80 to 400 inches of rain per year.

4. The weather in rain forests
   _____[remains]_____ the same all year long.

5. Some rain forests _____[have existed]_____
   for 70 million to 100 million years.

7

# 8. Identifying Compound Subjects and Predicates

A **compound subject** consists of more than one simple subject.

    <u>Beatrix Potter</u> and <u>Beverly Cleary</u> are famous children's authors.

A **compound predicate** consists of more than one simple predicate.

    Their books <u>amuse</u> and <u>delight</u> children everywhere.

**A.** Each sentence has a compound subject or predicate.
Draw a vertical line between the subject and the predicate.
Underline the compound subject or predicate.

1. The <u>owl</u> and the <u>pussycat</u> | went to sea
   in a beautiful pea-green boat.

2. The owl | <u>looked</u> up to the stars above
   and <u>sang</u> to a small guitar.

3. The <u>walrus</u> and the <u>carpenter</u> | were walking
   close at hand.

4. <u>Jack</u> and <u>Jill</u> | went up the hill for a pail of water.

5. Little Jack Horner | <u>stuck</u> in his thumb and <u>pulled</u> out a plum.

**B.** Read each sentence. Underline the compound subject(s).
Circle the compound predicate(s).

1. Beatrix Potter (wrote) and (illustrated) her own stories.

2. <u>Peter Rabbit</u> and his <u>family</u> are the characters in one story.

3. <u>Flopsy</u>, <u>Mopsy</u>, and <u>Cotton Tail</u> lived with Peter in a big fir tree.

4. <u>Mr. McGregor</u> and <u>Mrs. McGregor</u> (planted) and (weeded) their garden.

5. Mrs. Rabbit (shopped) for food and (cooked) the meals.

6. The three little bunnies (hopped) down the lane and (gathered) blackberries.

7. Peter (ran) away and (squeezed) under the gate.

8. Mr. McGregor (shouted) and (waved) his rake.

9. <u>Flopsy</u>, <u>Mopsy</u>, and <u>Cotton Tail</u> (ate) blackberries and (drank) milk.

10. <u>Peter</u> and his <u>mother</u> had tea for supper.

Name_____

# 9. Identifying Direct Objects

> The **direct object** is the noun or pronoun that completes the action of the verb.
> Many sentences need direct objects to complete their meaning. To find
> the direct object of a sentence, ask whom or what after the verb.
>
> | SUBJECT | VERB | DIRECT OBJECT | |
> |---------|------|---------------|---|
> | Our class | studied | Mexico | this year. |
> | The Aztecs in the lowlands | grew | squash. | |

**A.** Circle the direct object in each sentence.

1. The ancient Aztecs inhabited (Mexico).

2. Aztec farmers in the highlands grew (corn).

3. They traded the (corn) for things from the lowlands.

4. Aztec craftsmen made (jewelry) out of gold and silver.

5. Potters made beautiful (jars) out of clay.

6. The Aztecs did not have an (alphabet).

7. They used (pictographs) for their stories.

8. The Aztecs spoke (Nahuatl).

9. Some people in Mexico still speak
   this (language).

10. The Aztecs studied the (stars).

11. They developed a (calendar).

12. Their calendar had 260 (days) in a year.

13. The Aztecs built many magnificent (temples) to their gods.

14. The temples had the (shape) of pyramids.

15. We admire these ancient (people).

**B.** Complete each sentence by writing a direct object. [Answers will vary.]

1. Farmers in my state raise _____.

2. A factory near here manufactures _____.

3. People in my neighborhood speak _____.

4. I buy _____ at the supermarket.

5. I can make _____.

# 10. Identifying Indirect Objects

Some sentences have two objects—the direct object and the indirect object. The **indirect object** is the noun or pronoun that tells *to whom* or *for whom* the action is done.

I made a birthday cake for Jane.  =  I made Jane a birthday cake.
Carl gave a present to her.  =  Carl gave her a present.

**A.** Circle the indirect object in each sentence.
The direct object is underlined.

1. My aunt gave my cousin a surprise birthday party.

2. She sent my brother an invitation.

3. My brother showed my cousin the card.

4. My cousin told his mother the story.

5. My brother offered my aunt an apology.

6. The news reporter asked the politician a question about the schools.

7. The politician didn't give the reporter a very clear answer.

8. The reporter showed the audience a report about the schools.

9. The report denied teachers a pay raise.

10. The politician promised everyone a complete explanation.

**B.** Underline the direct object in each sentence.
Circle the indirect object.

1. Ms. Asbury gave each student an assignment.

2. Carol would sing the class a song.

3. The librarian showed Carol several songbooks.

4. Mike offered his classmate some help.

5. He taught Carol a song by Irving Berlin.

# 11. Reviewing Sentences

**A.** Decide whether each sentence is declarative, interrogative, imperative, or exclamatory. Write your answer on the line. Add the correct end punctuation.

_____[declarative]_____ 1. In 1346 Europeans heard of a terrible disease in China [.]

_____[declarative]_____ 2. At that time China was one of the world's busiest trading nations [.]

_____[declarative]_____ 3. The Black Sea was Europe's main link with China [.]

_____[imperative]_____ 4. Locate the Black Sea on a map [.]

_____[declarative]_____ 5. In October 1347 some ships reached Sicily from the Black Sea [.]

_____[declarative]_____ 6. Many sailors on board were dying of the Black Death [.]

_____[interrogative]_____ 7. What caused the Black Death [?]

_____[declarative]_____ 8. Rats carried the disease [.]

_____[declarative]_____ 9. Fleas bit the rats and then bit humans [.]

_____[interrogative]_____ 10. What was the disease like [?]

_____[declarative]_____ 11. People felt achy and vomited [.]

_____[declarative]_____ 12. They got black spots on their bodies [.]

_____[declarative]_____ 13. Death came very rapidly [.]

_____[exclamatory]_____ 14. Wow, *horrible* is the word for it [!]

_____[interrogative]_____ 15. How many people died of the Black Death [?]

_____[declarative]_____ 16. Almost one third of the people in Europe died within ten years [.]

_____[declarative]_____ 17. In some towns the dead outnumbered the living [.]

_____[exclamatory]_____ 18. That's unbelievable [!]

_____[imperative]_____ 19. Find out more about the Black Death [.]

_____[interrogative]_____ 20. Why couldn't doctors help the disease victims [?]

CONTINUED

**B.** Underline the compound subject(s) in each sentence.
Underline twice the compound predicate(s).

1. Birds, mammals, and reptiles live in Tanzania's Serengeti Park.

2. Elephants, buffaloes, and hippos ramble and eat the plains' grasses.

3. A bird with the odd name of the Bare-Faced Go-Away Bird runs and hops like a squirrel.

4. Crocodiles swim in the Grumeti River or bask on its banks.

5. Thousands of tourists visit the park each year and watch the animals.

**C.** Underline the direct object in each sentence.
Circle the indirect object.

1. The Serengeti provides the animals food and shelter.

2. Mother birds feed their babies insects.

3. Mother lions teach their cubs hunting skills.

4. The tall grass offers small animals hiding places.

5. The park rangers give visitors information about the animals.

## Try It Yourself
Write four sentences about a park or wildlife shelter near you.
Be sure each sentence is complete. Use correct punctuation.

_____

_____

_____

_____

## Check Your Own Work
Choose a piece of writing from your portfolio or journal, a work
in progress, an assignment from another class, or a letter.
Revise it, applying the skills you have reviewed.
The checklist will help you.

✔ Does each sentence express a complete thought?

✔ Does each sentence start with a capital letter?

✔ Does each sentence end with the correct punctuation mark?

# 12. Identifying Common and Proper Nouns

> A **noun** is a name word. A **proper noun** names a particular person, place, or thing. Proper nouns are capitalized.
>
> **Sylvester Stallone**     *Rocky*     **Philadelphia**     **Oscar**
>
> A **common noun** names one member of a group of persons, places, or things.
>
> **actor**          **movie**     **city**         **award**

**A.** Underline each noun. Above each noun write **P** if the noun is proper. Write **C** if the noun is common.

1. [P] Madeleine L'Engle has written many [C] books with exciting [C] adventures.

2. In [P] *Many Waters* the [C] writer invites her [C] readers on a fantastic [C] journey.

3. [P] Sandy Murry and [P] Dennys Murry are [C] twins.

4. Their [C] parents are [C] scientists who study the [C] planets.

5. [P] Mrs. Murry, their [C] mother, has a [C] laboratory near the [C] kitchen.

6. The two [C] teenagers find a [C] computer belonging to their [C] father.

7. The [C] keyboard has [C] characters in [P] Greek, [P] Russian, and [P] Hebrew.

8. [P] Sandy and [P] Dennys jokingly type in a [C] request for warmer [C] weather.

9. Suddenly there are a [C] fire, an [C] explosion—and endless [C] sand!

10. Are the [C] boys still on [P] Earth or in a different [C] galaxy?

**B.** Decide whether each noun is proper or common.
Write **P** if the noun is proper. Write **C** if the noun is common.
Then, for each proper noun write two related common nouns.
For each common noun write two related proper nouns.

|  | P/C | [Answers will vary.] |  |
|---|---|---|---|
| 1. English | [P] | _____ | _____ |
| 2. book | [C] | _____ | _____ |
| 3. Jupiter | [P] | _____ | _____ |
| 4. Sahara | [P] | _____ | _____ |
| 5. scientist | [C] | _____ | _____ |

# 13. Identifying Collective Nouns

A **collective noun** names a group of persons, animals, places, or things that are considered a unit. A collective noun usually takes a singular verb.

**My science <u>class</u> is very interesting.**
**A <u>group</u> of students does a demonstration every day.**

**A.** Underline the collective noun and circle the correct verb.

1. Crisscrossing the plains, the <u>herd</u> of buffalo ( search (searches) ) for grass to eat.

2. A <u>colony</u> of ants ( (is) are ) not a welcome sight at a picnic.

3. Is it true that a <u>school</u> of fish ( swim (swims) ) to the surface if it rains?

4. If a <u>hive</u> of bees ( grow (grows) ) large, half the bees will leave and make a new home.

5. A large <u>pride</u> of lions ( live (lives) ) in this area of the safari park.

6. A <u>club</u> ( put (puts) ) on a play at the school every year.

7. A <u>committee</u> of students and teachers ( choose (chooses) ) a play.

8. A <u>team</u> of students ( prepare (prepares) ) the costumes and props.

9. The <u>cast</u> ( (is) are ) made up of students from several schools.

10. The <u>audience</u> always ( give (gives) ) the students loud applause.

**B.** Write a collective noun for each word. [**Possible answers given.**]

1. scouts _____[troop]_____
2. players _____[team]_____
3. ships _____[fleet]_____
4. musicians _____[orchestra]_____
5. soldiers _____[army]_____

6. cards _____[deck]_____
7. singers _____[chorus]_____
8. students _____[class]_____
9. grapes _____[bunch]_____
10. turkeys _____[flock]_____

**C.** Write a sentence using each collective noun. [**Sentences will vary.**]

1. crew _____

2. jury _____

3. group _____

4. audience _____

5. committee _____

# 14. Identifying Concrete and Abstract Nouns

> A **concrete noun** names a thing that can be seen or touched.
>
> **The Greek temple is at the top of a mountain.**
>
> An **abstract noun** expresses a quality or a condition. It names something that cannot be seen or touched. Abstract nouns can be formed from other words by adding suffixes such as -dom, -hood, -ion, -tion, -ity, -ment, -ness, -ry, -ship, -th, and -ty.
>
> **Democracy had its origin in ancient Greece.**

**A.** Underline the concrete nouns in each sentence. Circle the abstract nouns.

1. Sparta and Athens were two city-states in ancient Greece.

2. The people of the two places had very different values and beliefs.

3. The people of Athens believed in freedom and democracy.

4. Athenians valued truth, beauty, and order.

5. The citizens erected beautiful buildings.

6. Plato, an Athenian philosopher, wrote about democratic principles.

7. However, Sparta was ruled by two kings.

8. The army was very important to Spartan government.

9. Spartans valued toughness and discipline.

10. Slaves in Sparta farmed the land and had few rights.

**B.** Write an abstract noun for each word by adding the proper suffix.
[Possible answers given.]

1. good _____[goodness]_____
2. brave _____[bravery]_____
3. friend _____[friendship]_____
4. king _____[kingdom/kingship]_____
5. grow _____[growth]_____

6. leader _____[leadership]_____
7. entertain _____[entertainment]_____
8. appreciate _____[appreciation]_____
9. accomplish _____[accomplishment]_____
10. honest _____[honesty]_____

# 15. Identifying Words Used as Nouns and Verbs

> A noun is a name word. A verb expresses action or being. Many words can be used as either nouns or verbs.
>
> NOUN
> **The study of planets reveals surprising facts.**
>
> VERB
> **Scientists study the planets.**

**A.** Above each underlined word write **N** if the word is a noun or **V** if it is a verb.

1. The [N] rings of Saturn are beautiful.

2. What material actually [V] rings the planet?

3. Tiny pieces of ice [V] form the rings.

4. Some pieces are tiny ice cubes, while others [V] reach the size of icebergs.

5. In 1655 a Dutch astronomer first saw these round [N] forms around Saturn.

6. Whenever possible, the spaceprobes [V] photograph the rings close-up.

7. It had the closest [N] view of the planet in history.

8. With telescopes scientists could [V] view only a few rings.

9. The [N] photographs showed many rings around Saturn, not just a few.

10. The spacecraft's photographs were a [N] surprise to scientists.

11. What could [V] cause Saturn's rings?

12. The [N] cause may have been an explosion of one of Saturn's moons.

13. Forces will slowly [V] pull the ice in the rings down into Saturn.

14. The [N] pull of gravity is one of these forces.

15. New facts about planets will [V] surprise scientists—and us—in the future.

**B.** Use each word in a sentence as a noun or a verb. The part of speech is indicated.

[Sentences will vary.]

1. study (noun) _____

2. surprise (verb)_____

3. photograph (noun) _____

4. cause (verb)_____

5. view (noun) _____

# 16. Identifying the Number of Nouns

A **singular noun** refers to one person, place, or thing.
A **plural noun** refers to more than one person, place, or thing.

| SINGULAR | PLURAL | | SINGULAR | PLURAL |
|----------|--------|---|----------|--------|
| computer | computers | | hoof | hooves |
| house | houses | | play | plays |
| princess | princesses | | story | stories |
| sheep | sheep | | tornado | tornadoes |

**Nouns**

**A.** Write the singular and plural forms of each noun.

SINGULAR        PLURAL

1. party     [party]         [parties]

2. pulley     [pulley]         [pulleys]

3. compass     [compass]         [compasses]

4. teeth     [tooth]         [teeth]

5. fish     [fish]         [fish]

6. calves     [calf]         [calves]

7. lives     [life]         [lives]

8. piano     [piano]         [pianos]

9. women     [woman]         [women]

10. potatoes     [potato]         [potatoes]

**B.** Complete each sentence with the plural form of the noun.

half     1. Pack both _____[halves]_____ of the watermelon in the cooler.

child     2. Many _____[children]_____ begin their education in preschool.

buggy     3. How many dune _____[buggies]_____ did your family rent?

tomato     4. Are _____[tomatoes]_____ considered fruits or vegetables?

refugee     5. The _____[refugees]_____ fled to a neighboring country.

# 17. Writing Plural Nouns

Complete each sentence with the plural form
of the noun at the left.

inventor    1. Thomas Edison is one of the most important
American _____[inventors]_____.

child    2. When he was young, he was different
from the other _____[children]_____.

question    3. He was curious and was always asking
_____[questions]_____.

patent    4. During his career he held over 1,000
_____[patents]_____.

assistant    5. Edison had a team of _____[assistants]_____ in his laboratory.

supply    6. He set up a kind of "invention factory," in which he gave his
workers materials and _____[supplies]_____ needed for research.

discovery    7. Two of his most famous _____[discoveries]_____ were the electric
light bulb and the phonograph record.

movie    8. The film and projectors used to make and show
_____[movies]_____ were also his ideas.

camera    9. Of course, he had invented movie _____[cameras]_____ too.

battery    10. He also developed a better way to make _____[batteries]_____.

torpedo    11. During World War I, he helped the U.S. Army find ways to protect
American ships from German _____[torpedoes]_____.

engine    12. He also invented better forms of electrical _____[engines]_____.
His first engine is in a museum, and it still works!

factory    13. He designed and built _____[factories]_____ to make chemicals,
cement, and phonograph records.

key    14. One of the _____[keys]_____ to Edison's success was reading:
Before he began a project, he read a lot about the subject.

day    15. Three _____[days]_____ after he died, much of America
dimmed its lights for one minute in his honor.

Thomas Edison always read as much as he could before
he started a new project. Give an example of a way you
can use reading to help you.

# 18. Identifying Nouns Used as Subjects

A noun can be the subject of a verb.
The **subject** tells what the sentence is about.

> The **Trojan War** is a legendary conflict between two ancient cities.
> During the Trojan War Greek **soldiers** from Sparta attacked Troy.

**A.** Underline the subject in each sentence.

1. <u>Menelaus</u> was the king of Sparta.

2. His wife's <u>name</u> was Helen.

3. His <u>wife</u> fell in love with a prince from Troy and went to Troy.

4. According to the legend, the <u>Greeks</u> started a war against Troy.

5. The <u>war</u> lasted more than 11 years.

6. Finally, a Greek <u>soldier</u> had an idea.

7. The <u>plan</u> was to build a large wooden statue of a horse.

8. Greek <u>soldiers</u> hid in the horse.

9. The Greek <u>army</u> left the horse near the gates of Troy and sailed away.

10. The <u>people</u> found the statue and took it into the city.

11. A <u>woman</u> of Troy tried to warn the people about the statue.

12. Cassandra's <u>warnings</u> were ignored.

13. The Greeks' <u>ships</u> returned that night.

14. The <u>troops</u> inside the horse came out and opened the city gates.

15. <u>Troy</u> lost the war because of this surprise attack by the Greeks.

**B.** Use each noun as the subject of a sentence. [Sentences will vary.]

1. Greece _____

2. Troy _____

3. soldiers _____

4. Cassandra _____

5. the Trojan horse _____

# 19. Identifying Nouns Used as Subject Complements

> A **subject complement** is a noun that completes the meaning of a linking verb in a sentence. It renames or describes the subject.
>
> **Japan is a country in Asia.**
> **(Japan = country)**

**A.** Underline the subject complements.

1. Japan is a nation of islands.

2. Korea, China, and Russia are the nearest neighbors of Japan.

3. The capital of Japan is Tokyo.

4. Tokyo is a large, densely populated city.

5. The official language of the country is Japanese.

6. In the Japanese language the country's name is not Japan.

7. The name of the country in Japanese is Nippon.

8. Of Japan's four major islands, Honshu is the biggest island.

9. Many of the Japanese people are farmers and fishers.

10. Rice is an important crop of Japan.

11. Canned and fresh fish are important products.

12. However, Japan is not primarily an agricultural country.

13. Japan is a major industrial nation.

14. The country is a major producer of cars, electronics, and motorcycles.

15. In fact, Japan is a world economic power.

**B.** Circle the subject in each sentence.
Underline the subject complement.

1. Japan is a mountainous country.

2. Some mountains are volcanoes.

3. The most famous volcano in Japan is Mount Fuji.

4. This mountain is the subject of many paintings and photographs.

5. A climb to the top of Mount Fuji is an important goal of many Japanese.

# 20. Identifying Nouns Used in Direct Address

> A noun in direct address names the person spoken to.
>
> **The Civil War, <u>Jenny</u>, lasted four years.**
> **<u>Mark</u>, what was the capital of the Confederacy?**

**A.** Underline the noun(s) in direct address.

1. <u>Students</u>, please look at the map of the United States during the Civil War.

2. Before the Civil War, <u>Frank</u>, the United States had 33 states.

3. Eleven states joined the Confederacy, <u>Eddie</u> and <u>Joe</u>.

4. Twenty-two states, <u>Carolyn</u>, stayed in the Union.

5. <u>Class</u>, West Virginia broke off from Virginia and joined the Union too.

6. <u>Frank</u>, did the Civil War begin in 1865?

7. Were slaves freed during the war, <u>boys</u> and <u>girls</u>?

8. <u>Wendy</u>, was New York on the side of the North?

9. <u>Chen</u>, was Lincoln president during the Civil War?

10. Did the South win the Civil War, <u>Mr. Livingston</u>?

**B.** Complete each sentence with a noun or nouns in direct address. Insert commas where needed. [Answers will vary.]

1. _____ have you visited the Civil War exhibit at the museum?

2. The Civil War _____ divided the loyalties of many families.

3. One result of the Civil War was the end of slavery in the United States _____.

4. _____ the first battle of the Civil War took place in Fort Sumter, South Carolina.

5. The Civil War ended when General Lee surrendered at Appomatox _____.

# 21. Identifying Appositives

> An **appositive** is a noun that follows another noun. It renames or describes the noun it follows.
>
> **The Continental Congress, a group of American patriots, played a key role in the American colonies' fight for independence.**
>
> **(Continental Congress = group)**

**A.** Circle the noun in apposition in each sentence.
Underline the noun it renames or describes.

1. Thomas Jefferson, a patriot from Virginia, wrote much of the Declaration of Independence.

2. John Hancock, the president of the Continental Congress, was the first signer of the Declaration of Independence.

3. George III, the king of England, sent troops to the colonies.

4. The Battle of Lexington, the first armed fight during the American Revolution, took place on April 19, 1775.

5. George Washington, the first president of the United States, commanded the army during the Revolutionary War.

6. The Marquis de Lafayette, a French aristocrat, traveled to America to help the colonists during the Revolutionary War.

7. Paul Revere, a patriot and silversmith, warned the people of Massachusetts that British troops were going to attack soon.

8. The Redcoats, the British soldiers, could not defeat the colonists.

9. General Cornwallis, the leader of the British troops, lost several battles.

10. Yorktown, the last important battle of the war, was won by the Americans on October 17, 1781.

**B.** Complete each sentence with a noun in apposition. [Possible answers given.]

1. Springfield, a _____[city]_____ in central Illinois, is the capital of the state.

2. Abraham Lincoln, the sixteenth _____[president]_____ of the United States, lived in Springfield.

3. The Lincoln Home, the only _____[house]_____ Lincoln ever owned, is a national historic site.

4. The Lincoln-Herndon Offices, the _____[building]_____ where Lincoln worked as a lawyer for ten years, can also be visited by tourists.

5. One of the most-visited cemeteries in the United States is Oak Ridge Cemetery, the _____[place]_____ with Lincoln's tomb.

# 22. Reviewing the Uses of Nouns

**A.** Write the use of each underlined noun on the line. Use the key below.

| SUBJECT | SUBJECT COMPLEMENT | DIRECT ADDRESS | APPOSITIVE |
|---|---|---|---|
| S | SC | DA | App |

_[S]_ 1. <u>Scientists</u> have identified about one million kinds of insects.

_[SC]_ 2. Beetles are the largest <u>group</u> of insects.

_[SC]_ 3. The head, thorax, and abdomen are the three <u>parts</u> of an insect's body.

_[App]_ 4. The thorax, the <u>part</u> behind an insect's head, has the insect's legs.

_[DA]_ 5. Insects, <u>Ava</u>, are found throughout the world.

_[App]_ 6. The water strider, an unusual <u>insect</u>, lives in the sea.

_[DA]_ 7. The mayfly, <u>Ray</u>, sometimes lives for only two hours.

_[S]_ 8. Some <u>termites</u> live up to fifty years.

_[App]_ 9. Metamorphosis, a <u>change</u> in form, characterizes the growth of many insects.

_[SC]_ 10. Egg, larva, pupa, and adult are the four <u>stages</u> in metamorphosis.

**B.** Underline all the nouns used as subjects, subject complements, appositives, or in direct address. Write the correct code from Part A above for each noun you underline.

1. Some [S]<u>insects</u> are [SC]<u>pests</u>.

2. These [S]<u>insects</u> may eat crops and plants.

3. The [S]<u>termite</u>, a [App]<u>pest</u>, destroys wood.

4. Some [S]<u>insects</u> are [SC]<u>carriers</u> of diseases.

5. The [S]<u>honeybee</u>, a useful [App]<u>insect</u>, is a [SC]<u>pollinator</u> of plants.

6. [S]<u>Honeybees</u> and [S]<u>ants</u> are social [SC]<u>insects</u>.

7. [DA]<u>Carla</u>, do [S]<u>honeybees</u> and [S]<u>ants</u> live in groups?

8. [S]<u>Grasshoppers</u> are a [SC]<u>food</u> in many places.

9. One useful [S]<u>product</u> from insects is [SC]<u>honey</u>.

10. [S]<u>Silk</u> is another [SC]<u>product</u> from insects.

23

# 23. Forming the Possessive Case

---

A **possessive form of a noun** expresses ownership.

SINGULAR POSSESSIVE       PLURAL POSSESSIVE

the student's computer       the students' computers

---

**Nouns**

**A.** Write the singular possessive, the plural, and the plural possessive for each singular noun.

| SINGULAR | SINGULAR POSSESSIVE | PLURAL | PLURAL POSSESSIVE |
|---|---|---|---|
| 1. turkey | [turkey's] | [turkeys] | [turkeys'] |
| 2. neighbor | [neighbor's] | [neighbors] | [neighbors'] |
| 3. driver | [driver's] | [drivers] | [drivers'] |
| 4. sheep | [sheep's] | [sheep] | [sheep's] |
| 5. child | [child's] | [children] | [children's] |
| 6. fox | [fox's] | [foxes] | [foxes'] |
| 7. teacher | [teacher's] | [teachers] | [teachers'] |
| 8. woman | [woman's] | [women] | [women's] |
| 9. man | [man's] | [men] | [men's] |
| 10. sister-in-law | [sister-in-law's] | [sisters-in-law] | [sisters-in-law's] |

**B.** Rewrite each phrase, using the possessive case.

1. the orders of the coach     [the coach's orders]

2. a delay of an hour     [an hour's delay]

3. the home of my parents     [my parents' home]

4. the books of the teacher     [the teacher's books]

5. the toys of the children     [the children's toys]

# 24. Working with the Possessive Case

**A.** Complete each sentence with the possessive form of the noun.

pilot        1. A _____[pilot's]_____ training requires
             long hours of hard study.

Sally        2. _____[Sally's]_____ running shoes
             are in the upstairs closet.

soldiers     3. We listened to the rhythmic sound of the
             _____[soldiers']_____ feet as they marched.

Mrs. Riddle  4. Tina and Sue washed _____[Mrs. Riddle's]_____ car.

boys         5. The _____[boys']_____ books are in their backpacks.

women        6. _____[Women's]_____ coats are on sale this week
             in the department store in the mall.

Thomas       7. Did you find _____[Thomas's]_____ in-line skates?

brother-in-law 8. On Thanksgiving we tasted my _____[brother-in-law's]_____ special
             recipe for sweet potatoes.

deer         9. The _____[deer's]_____ large antlers show that it is quite old.

guards       10. The security _____[guards']_____ office is near the exit
             to the parking lot.

**B.** Rewrite each phrase, using a possessive noun.

1. the request of the librarian       [the librarian's request]

2. the work of the scientist          [the scientist's work]

3. the diagnosis of the doctor         [the doctor's diagnosis]

4. the bicycles of the girls           [the girls' bicycles]

5. the cell phones of the workers      [the workers' cell phones]

6. the shouts of the children          [the children's shouts]

7. the pen of Mr. James                [Mr. James's pen]

8. the red feathers of the cardinals   [the cardinals' red feathers]

9. the statements of the witnesses     [the witnesses' statements]

10. the suitcases of the guests        [the guests' suitcases]

Nouns

Name_____

# 25. Identifying Nouns Used as Direct Objects

> A noun can be used as the direct object of a verb. A direct object answers the question whom or what after the verb.
>
> | VERB | DIRECT OBJECT | | VERB | DIRECT OBJECT |
>
> Britain *acquired* Hong Kong in the 1800s. It *ruled* the colony until 1997.

Nouns

**A.** Circle the direct object(s) in each sentence. The verbs are underlined.

1. Hong Kong includes 200 islands off the south coast of China.

2. Britain leased this territory from China in 1898.

3. Hong Kong reclaimed land from the sea for more space.

4. Hong Kong traded goods with the rest of China until 1949.

5. At that time Britain forbade trade with Communist China.

6. Since the 1960s Hong Kong has manufactured radios and other electronics.

7. For more than 30 years China requested the return of Hong Kong.

8. Britain officially returned this land to China on July 1, 1997.

9. Officially the People's Republic of China governs Hong Kong now.

10. By Chinese law Hong Kong will have a capitalist economy for the next 50 years.

**B.** Underline the verb in each sentence. Circle the direct object(s).

1. An emperor of China, Qin Shi Huang, began the Great Wall in 221 B.C.

2. The builders used brick, stone, and earth for the wall.

3. The wall protected the country's border.

4. The wall kept enemies out of China.

5. Guards on the wall built fires.

6. The fire smoke warned people about enemies in the area.

7. Recently, through the use of satellites, scientists studied the wall.

8. With the satellite data, they discovered more sections below ground.

9. A new Great Wall would cost $260 billion dollars in today's money.

10. Today the wall amazes tourists from all over the world.

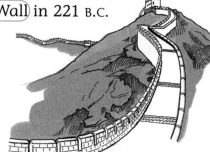

# 26. Identifying Nouns Used as Objects of Prepositions

> Prepositions show time, direction, place, and relationship. Some common prepositions are *in, into, on, to, by, for, from, at, with,* and *without.* The noun that follows a preposition in a prepositional phrase is called the object of the preposition.
>
> | PREPOSITION | OBJECT | PREPOSITION | OBJECT |
> |---|---|---|---|
> | **Venice is located *on*** | **islands** | **that are *in* the** | **Adriatic Sea.** |

**A.** Circle each object of the preposition. The prepositions are underlined.

1. Venice is a city in Italy, a country of southern Europe.
2. Venice was an important port during the Middle Ages.
3. Venetian merchants traded with many different countries.
4. Venetian ships traveled between Italy and the Middle East.
5. Marco Polo, the famous explorer of China, was from Venice.
6. Today Venice is famous for beautiful buildings.
7. The Rialto Bridge passes over the Grand Canal in the center of the city.
8. Cars cannot drive into Venice, and so outside the city is a parking lot.
9. People travel through the city on vaporettos, which are water buses.
10. Tourists ride in gondolas, small boats paddled by large oars.

**B.** Complete each sentence with prepositions. [**Possible answers given.**]

1. ____[In]____ 1271 Marco Polo traveled ____[to]____ China.
2. ____[On]____ the trip they passed ____[through]____ Turkey, Iran, and Afghanistan.
3. They traveled ____[by]____ boat, ____[on/by]____ foot, and ____[on]____ camels.
4. Marco Polo stayed ____[in]____ China ____[for]____ 17 years.
5. He met people ____[in]____ China, India, Mongolia, and other countries.
6. He worked ____[for]____ the emperor ____[of]____ China, Kublai Khan.
7. After returning ____[to]____ Italy, he wrote a book ____[on/about]____ the trip.
8. Many people ____[in]____ Italy didn't believe Marco Polo's amazing stories ____[of/about]____ China.
9. Marco Polo's book has been translated ____[into]____ many languages.
10. Marco Polo may be the most famous traveler ____[in]____ the history ____[of]____ the world!

# 27. Identifying Nouns Used as Indirect Objects

> A noun can be used as the indirect object of a verb.
> The indirect object tells *to whom* or *for whom* the action was done.
>
> | VERB | INDIRECT OBJECT | DIRECT OBJECT |
> |------|-----------------|---------------|
> | Iris *taught* | **the old dog** | **new *tricks*.** |

**Nouns**

**A.** Underline the verb in each sentence. Circle the indirect object. The direct object is italicized.

1. The hospital volunteer <u>read</u> the (patient) a *story*.
2. The school committee <u>awarded</u> (Marjorie) a *prize* for her essay.
3. Mrs. Jones <u>bought</u> her (son) a new *bicycle*.
4. I <u>sent</u> the (editor) a *letter* about a new park for our neighborhood.
5. The museum <u>offered</u> the (owner) a million *dollars* for the painting.
6. The soloist <u>sang</u> the (audience) a beautiful *ballad*.
7. Mrs. Williamson <u>told</u> the (children) a *story* about visiting the Kremlin.
8. The music teacher <u>taught</u> the (class) a patriotic *song*.
9. George Washington always <u>told</u> (people) the *truth*.
10. Tyrone <u>gave</u> his (mother) some *roses* on Mother's Day.

**B.** Complete each sentence with an indirect object. Underline the direct object. [**Possible answers given.**]

1. The teacher gave _____[the students]_____ their homework <u>assignment</u>.
2. The United States Constitution ensures _____[people]_____ the <u>right</u> to vote.
3. The movie star sent _____[the fan]_____ an autographed <u>picture</u>.
4. Their father promised _____[the children]_____ <u>pizza</u> for dinner.
5. Ms. Gibbs was dissatisfied with the service at the hotel, so she wrote _____[the manager]_____ a <u>letter</u> of complaint.
6. The press secretary handed _____[the clerk]_____ a <u>copy</u> of the president's speech.
7. Mr. Glass sent _____[the bookstore owner]_____ an <u>order</u> for 10 books.
8. The instructor taught _____[the student]_____ the <u>rules</u> of the road.
9. The guide showed _____[the tourists]_____ the <u>desk</u> where the president worked.
10. The usher offered _____[the patron]_____ a <u>program</u> with information about the play.

# 28. Identifying Appositives

A subject, a direct object, an indirect object, or an object of a preposition can have an appositive.

> **Thomas Jefferson, a lawyer, occupied many public offices.**
> **He designed his own home, Monticello.**
> **The Continental Congress gave Thomas Jefferson, a good writer, the job of drafting a declaration of independence.**
> **I am reading about Thomas Jefferson, our third president.**

Underline the appositive in each sentence. Circle the noun it explains.

1. Thomas Jefferson studied law at the College of William and Mary, a school in Virginia.

2. He was appointed to the Second Continental Congress, the colonies' representative body, in 1775.

3. In 1776 Jefferson wrote the Declaration of Independence, a key document of American history.

4. The Declaration of Independence contained a long list of complaints about George III, the king of England.

5. In 1784 Jefferson agreed to succeed the American ambassador to France, Benjamin Franklin.

6. Because Jefferson did not like to speak in public, he gave only two speeches, his inaugural addresses, as president.

7. He even made the State of the Union address, an annual report to Congress from the president, in writing.

8. Usually he did not meet in person with the cabinet, his political advisors.

9. Cabinet members sent him memos, summaries of their recommendations.

10. The Louisiana Purchase, the most important event in his presidency, occurred in 1803.

11. Jefferson bought the territory from Napoleon, the leader of France.

12. Jefferson ordered his private secretary, Meriwether Lewis, to explore the new land.

13. Jefferson paid a very low price, $15 million dollars, for the territory.

14. After he left the presidency, Jefferson turned his attention to another interest, architecture.

15. Jefferson designed two new projects, the campus of the University of Virginia and a house in Bedford, Virginia.

# 29. Reviewing Nouns Used as Objects and Appositives

**A.** On the line write the use of each underlined noun. Use the key below.

| DIRECT OBJECT | INDIRECT OBJECT | OBJECT OF PREPOSITION | APPOSITIVE |
|---|---|---|---|
| DO | IO | OP | App |

**[DO]** 1. Comic strips tell <u>stories</u> in a series of pictures.

**[OP]** 2. Most comic strips appear in <u>newspapers</u>.

**[DO]** 3. Cartoonists draw the <u>pictures</u>.

**[App]** 4. A cartoonist generally works for a syndicate, a <u>company</u> that acts as an agent.

**[IO]** 5. Syndicates sell <u>newspapers</u> the completed comic strips.

**[OP]** 6. Many famous characters first appeared in the <u>comics</u>.

**[OP]** 7. Charles Schulz created *Peanuts* with <u>Charlie Brown</u> and <u>Snoopy</u>.

**[App]** 8. Other famous comic strip characters are Dick Tracy, a <u>detective</u>, and Tarzan.

**[DO]** 9. Comics have inspired <u>books</u>, <u>movies</u>, and TV <u>programs</u>.

**[IO]** 10. Comics give <u>readers</u> some good laughs, and that is why they're called the funnies.

**B.** Underline the nouns used as objects and appositives.
Write the appropriate code from Part A above each noun you underline.

1. The first comic, *Hogan's Alley* **[App]**, appeared in a <u>newspaper</u> **[OP]** in <u>1895</u> **[OP]**.

2. Richard F. Outcault illustrated the <u>comic</u> **[DO]**.

3. Outcault gave the <u>world</u> **[IO]** its first comic <u>character</u> **[DO]**.

4. The cartoon starred a <u>character</u> **[DO]** by the <u>name</u> **[OP]** of the <u>Yellow</u> **[OP]** Kid.

5. It was published by *The World* **[OP]**, a New York <u>newspaper</u> **[App]**, on <u>Sundays</u> **[OP]**.

**C.** Write a sentence using each noun as indicated in parentheses. **[Possible answers given.]**

1. comics (DO) _____ [Do you read the comics on Sunday?] _____

2. Snoopy (OP) _____ [Charlie Brown was a friend of Snoopy.] _____

3. children (IO) _____ [Aunt Maya gave the children comic books.] _____

4. newspaper (OP) _____ [I save the comics section of the newspaper.] _____

5. a comic strip character (App) _____ [Hobbes, a comic strip character, is a tiger.]

# 30. Reviewing Nouns

**A.** Identify the underlined nouns.
In column 1 write **C** for common or **P** for proper.
In column 2, write **C** if the noun is a collective noun.
In column 3, write **A** for abstract or **C** for concrete.

|  | 1 | 2 | 3 |
|---|---|---|---|
| 1. Japan is a <u>democracy</u>. | [C] | | [A] |
| 2. The <u>Diet</u>, a kind of parliament, is its legislative body. | [P] | [C] | [A] |
| 3. Japan has a large <u>fleet</u> of modern fishing boats. | [C] | [C] | [C] |
| 4. <u>Hondas</u> are imported from Japan. | [P] | | [C] |
| 5. <u>Respect</u> for the elderly is an important Japanese value. | [C] | | [A] |

**B.** Write the singular possessive and the plural possessive of each word.

|  | SINGULAR POSSESSIVE | PLURAL POSSESSIVE |
|---|---|---|
| 1. country | [country's] | [countries'] |
| 2. child | [child's] | [children's] |
| 3. citizen | [citizen's] | [citizens'] |
| 4. sheep | [sheep's] | [sheep's] |
| 5. emperor | [emperor's] | [emperors'] |

**C.** Write on the line how each underlined noun is used. Use the key below.

| SUBJECT | SUBJECT COMPLEMENT | DIRECT ADDRESS | APPOSITIVE |
|---|---|---|---|
| S | SC | DA | App |

[SC] 1. Tokyo is the <u>capital</u> of Japan.

[S] 2. <u>Sapporo</u> is a winter resort in northern Japan.

[S] 3. Every day speedy bullet <u>trains</u> cross Japan.

[App] 4. The emperor of Japan, <u>Emperor Akihito</u>, is the nominal head of state.

[DA] 5. The prime minister, <u>Elaine</u>, is the head of the Japanese government.

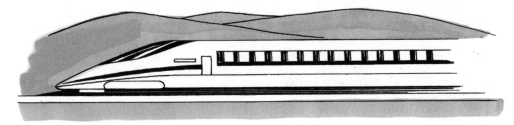

**Nouns**

**D.** The underlined nouns are used as objects or appositives.
Write on the line how each is used. Use the key below.

| DIRECT OBJECT | INDIRECT OBJECT | OBJECT OF PREPOSITION | APPOSITIVE |
|---|---|---|---|
| DO | IO | OP | App |

__[DO]__ 1. The fox wanted the <u>grapes</u> in the crow's beak.

__[App]__ 2. A good plan was created by the fox, a very clever <u>animal</u>.

__[DO]__ 3. He praised the <u>crow</u> for its lovely songs.

__[OP]__ 4. Because the crow opened its beak for a song, the grapes fell
into the fox's <u>paws</u>.

__[IO]__ 5. The story teaches <u>readers</u> a lesson about flattery.

**E.** Write on the line how each underlined noun in each sentence is used.
Use the key below.

| DIRECT OBJECT | SUBJECT COMPLEMENT | DIRECT ADDRESS | INDIRECT OBJECT | APPOSITIVE |
|---|---|---|---|---|
| DO | SC | DA | IO | App |

__[SC]__ 1. Fables are short <u>stories</u> that illustrate a lesson.

__[App]__ 2. Aesop, an ancient <u>Greek</u>, is the author of a number of fables.

__[DO]__ 3. Aesop wrote "<u>The Fox and the Grapes</u>."

__[IO]__ 4. Many parents read their <u>children</u> fables at bedtime.

__[DA]__ 5. What is your favorite fable, <u>Kevin</u>?

## Try It Yourself

Write three sentences about a country or place that interests you.
Be sure that each sentence has a subject. Try to use appositives.

_____

_____

_____

## Check Your Own Work

Choose a selection from your writing portfolio, your journal, a work in progress,
an assignment from another class, or a letter. Revise it, applying the skills you
have reviewed. The checklist will help you.

✔ Do all the sentences have subjects?

✔ Have you capitalized all proper nouns?

✔ Have you used the correct forms of plurals?

✔ Have you used apostrophes correctly with the possessive case?

✔ Have you used commas with appositives and nouns in direct address?

# 31. Identifying Personal Pronouns

> A **pronoun** is a word that takes the place of a noun.
> A **personal pronoun** shows the speaker (first person):
> *I, me, we, us*; the person spoken to (second person):
> *you*; the person, place, or thing spoken of (third person):
> *he, she, it, him, her, they, them*.
>
> **FIRST PERSON**
> <u>I</u> am reading a book about Angelina Grimké.
>
> **SECOND PERSON**
> Do <u>you</u> know who she is?
>
> **THIRD PERSON**
> <u>She</u> crusaded against slavery before the Civil War.

Underline the personal pronoun(s) in each sentence.
Write the person of each pronoun above it.
Use the key below.

| FIRST PERSON | SECOND PERSON | THIRD PERSON |
|:---:|:---:|:---:|
| 1 | 2 | 3 |

ANGELINA

1. [1] <u>I</u> learned about Angelina and Sarah Grimké;
[3] <u>they</u> were crusaders against slavery.

2. Slavery seemed terrible to [3] <u>them</u>, and
so [3] <u>they</u> wanted to help end [3] <u>it</u>.

3. The sisters wrote articles about slavery and
published [3] <u>them</u> in newspapers and magazines.

4. [3] <u>They</u> told Southern women, "[2] <u>You</u> should talk
to your husbands and friends about slavery.
Tell [3] <u>them</u> that [2] <u>you</u> think [3] <u>it</u> is wrong."

5. [1] <u>I</u> think that [1] <u>we</u> owe a lot to people like
Sarah Grimké and Angelina Grimké because
[3] <u>they</u> helped [1] <u>us</u> in the fight for human rights.

SARAH

**Angelina and Sarah Grimké fought for the rights of others.
Give an example of something you can do to help others in
their struggle for human rights.**

# 32. Understanding Number and Gender of Personal Pronouns

> A pronoun is singular when it refers to one person, place, or thing.
> **Tom** sent an *e-mail* to his *mother*.
> <u>He</u> sent <u>it</u> to <u>her</u>.
>
> A pronoun is plural when it refers to more than one person, place, or thing.
> **Tonya and Maria** brought some *cookies*.
> <u>They</u> brought <u>them</u>.
>
> **Third person singular pronoun** can be masculine, feminine, or neuter.
> MASCULINE  FEMININE                              NEUTER
> <u>He</u> helped <u>her</u> prepare supper. I helped eat <u>it</u>.

**A.** Underline the personal pronoun(s) in each sentence. Above each write **S** if it is singular and **P** if it is plural.

1. My brother and <u>I</u> love to travel. [S]

2. Last year <u>we</u> took a trip to London. [P]

3. <u>It</u> is a beautiful and historic city. [S]

4. My brother went to see the changing of the guards, and <u>he</u> got his picture taken standing next to two of <u>them</u>. [S] [P]

5. We bought fish and chips every day and ate <u>them</u> for lunch. [P]

**B.** Write on the line a pronoun that could take the place of the underlined word(s). Then on the same line identify the gender of each third person singular pronoun you write. Write **M** if it is masculine, **F** if it is feminine, and **N** if it is neuter.

____[They]____ 1. <u>Susan and Sam</u> love to travel with their parents.

____[They]____ 2. The two <u>children</u> went to London last year.

____[It, N]____ 3. <u>London</u> is the capital of England.

____[She, F]____ 4. <u>Susan</u> enjoyed seeing the crown jewels.

____[He, M]____ 5. <u>Sam</u> saw some old weapons at the Tower of London.

____[it, N]____ 6. They saw Big Ben and were impressed by the big <u>clock</u>.

____[them]____ 7. Sam took photographs of the <u>Tower and Big Ben</u>.

____[them]____ 8. I got a beautiful postcard from <u>Susan and Sam</u>.

____[We]____ 9. The postcard said, "<u>Susan and I</u> are having a great time."

____[us]____ 10. They brought souvenirs for my <u>brother and me</u>.

Name_____

# 33. Using Pronouns as Subjects

> A personal pronoun can be used as a subject of a sentence.
> The **subject pronouns** are *I, we, you, he, she, it,* and *they.*
>> <u>I</u> saw the White House on the news last night.
>> <u>It</u> is a really beautiful building.

Circle the correct pronoun in parentheses.

1. Jill, Mark, and ( (I) me ) prepared a report on Washington, D.C.

2. ( (We) Us ) did research on the Internet and at the library.

3. Pierre L'Enfant designed the city. ( Him (He) ) was from France.

4. The city was named for George Washington.
   ( (He) Him ) hired L'Enfant to design it.

5. The White House is the home of the president.
   ( (It) They ) has been the home of every
   American president since John Adams.

6. Thomas Jefferson entered the contest for the design of
   the White House. However, ( him (he) ) did not win.

7. Dolley Madison was the wife of President James Madison. ( (She) Her )
   rescued papers from the White House before the British burned it in 1814.

8. First Lady Jacqueline Kennedy made important contributions to the White House.
   ( (She) Her ) redecorated it with antiques and old paintings.

9. The Washington Monument honors the nation's first president.
   ( (It) They ) opened to the public in 1885.

10. Members of the House of Representatives meet in the Capitol. The senators
    and ( (they) them ) form the legislative branch of the government.

11. The John F. Kennedy Center for the Performing Arts is in Washington, D.C.
    ( They (It) ) has theaters for concerts, drama, and opera.

12. ( (You) Me ) can visit many places in Washington, D.C., including the
    White House, the Capitol, and the Smithsonian Institution.

13. My family and ( (I) me ) visited Washington, D.C., last summer.

14. I think that ( (it) she ) is a really beautiful city.

15. What do ( (you) me ) want to see when you visit Washington, D.C.?

35

# 34. Using Pronouns as Subject Complements

> A subject complement follows a verb of being and refers to the same person as the subject of the sentence. A **subject pronoun** can replace a noun used as a subject complement.
>
> **The editor of the school paper is <u>she</u>.**
> **It is <u>I</u> who washed all the dishes.**

**A.** Circle the correct pronoun in parentheses.

1. The assistant editors are Kristen and ( (she) her ).

2. It was ( her (she) ) who wrote that funny story in this issue of the paper.

3. It was ( (he) him ) who drew the cartoon that illustrated the story.

4. The photographers for the paper are Jason and ( (they) them ).

5. The page designers are Allison and ( me (I) ).

6. "Is that you, Joel?" "Yes, it is ( (I) me )."

7. "Who told you that joke, Elaine?" "It was ( him (he) )."

8. "Hello. Is Alex there?" "Yes, this is ( (he) him )."

9. "Who is the girl in the third row? Is it Alice?" "Yes, it's ( her (she) )."

10. "Are those your friends waving at us?" "Yes, it is ( (they) them )."

11. I am sure that it wasn't ( us (we) ) who left the door open.

12. It was ( (they) them ) who left the dishes and cups on the table.

13. The children playing football on the lawn were Susan and ( (she) her ).

14. It was ( them (they) ) who rang the doorbell in the middle of the night.

15. Many people think that I am ( her (she) ).

**B.** Complete each sentence with a personal pronoun. Vary your choices. **[Answers will vary.]**

1. The first ones to cross the finish line were _____.

2. The student who will sing onstage is _____.

3. Are you sure it was _____ in the gym?

4. It was _____ who were on television.

5. Was it _____ in the skeleton costume?

# 35. Reviewing Subject Pronouns

**A.** Circle the correct personal pronoun in parentheses. On the line write **S** if it is used as a subject or **SC** if it is used as a subject complement.

___[S]___ 1. Nicholas II was the last czar of imperial Russia, and ( (he) him ) ruled the country from 1895 to 1917.

___[S]___ 2. ( Him (He) ) was married to Alexandra.

___[S]___ 3. ( (She) Her ) was called the czarina.

___[S]___ 4. ( (They) Them ) got married in 1894 and had five children.

___[SC]___ 5. Nicholas was not a good leader. It was ( (he) him ) who was responsible for many of Russia's problems.

___[S]___ 6. The government was not good. ( (It) Them ) was very corrupt, and the people were poor and had little freedom.

___[SC]___ 7. Alexandra became a center of controversy. It was ( (she) her ) who fell under the influence of Rasputin.

___[S]___ 8. ( (He) Him ) promised to cure her son with his magic powers.

___[S]___ 9. ( (She) Her ) let Rasputin get influence over the government.

___[SC]___ 10. Russian nobles hated Rasputin. The people who decided to stop Rasputin were ( (they) them ).

___[SC]___ 11. Conditions in Russia became worse, and revolutionaries plotted against the czar. It was ( them (they) ) who ruled next.

___[S]___ 12. The revolutionaries forced Nicholas to resign his throne. Then ( him (he) ) and his family were taken to Siberia and killed.

___[S]___ 13. However, years later a woman in England came forward. ( Her (She) ) said she was the czar's daughter, Anastasia.

___[SC]___ 14. Many thought that the czar's daughter was ( her (she) ).

___[S]___ 15. Today scientists have found the grave of the czar's family. ( (They) Them ) say that one of the people in the grave is Anastasia.

**B.** Write on the line a personal pronoun in place of the underlined word or phrase.

___[They]___ 1. <u>Nicholas and Alexandra</u> were the last rulers of imperial Russia.

___[she]___ 2. It was <u>Alexandra</u> who was married to Nicholas.

___[he]___ 3. It was <u>Nicholas II</u> who gave up his throne in 1917.

___[she]___ 4. Sadly, <u>Anastasia</u> died with the rest of her family in Russia.

___[they]___ 5. The people who then ruled Russia were <u>revolutionaries</u>.

**Pronouns**

# 36. Using Pronouns as Direct Objects

> A personal pronoun can be used as the direct object of a verb.
> The **object pronouns** are *me, us, you, him, her, it,* and *them.*
>
> **Julius Caesar was a ruler of Rome.**
> **His enemies killed <u>him</u> in 44 B.C.**

**Pronouns**

**A.** Circle the correct pronoun in parentheses.

1. Julius Caesar was a leader in the Roman army.
   He joined ( (it) him ) as a young man.

2. He met a woman, Calpurnia, from a wealthy
   family and married ( she (her) ) in 59 B.C.

3. The Romans first selected ( he (him) ) for
   public office in 74 B.C.

4. Caesar went to Gaul—modern France—and conquered ( (it) them ).

5. Caesar had enemies in Rome. He defeated ( they (them) ) in 45 B.C.
   and took over the government.

6. As a ruler, Caesar reformed the calendar. We still use ( them (it) ) today
   in a modified version.

7. The Romans honored ( he (him) ) by naming July after him.

8. His stories about his battles survive, and people still read ( (them) they ).

9. Caesar's enemies killed ( he (him) ) on March 15, 44 B.C.

10. On Caesar's death, Antony and Octavian succeeded ( (him) he ).

**B.** Use a personal pronoun to replace the words in parentheses.

1. Cleopatra ruled ___[it]___ (Egypt) from 51 to 30 B.C.

2. Cleopatra met ___[him]___ (Mark Antony) in 46 B.C.

3. He fell in love with Cleopatra, and he married ___[her]___ (Cleopatra).

4. Antony and Cleopatra wanted more power, and this angered
   ___[them]___ (the Romans).

5. Octavian went to Egypt and defeated Antony and ___[her]___ (Cleopatra).
   The pair of lovers killed themselves.

Name_____

# 37. Using Pronouns as Objects of Prepositions

> An object pronoun can be used as the object of a preposition.
>
> **The teacher wanted to talk to <u>me</u> about my science fair project.**

**A.** Circle the correct pronoun in parentheses.

1. Yesterday the coach read some basic basketball rules to ( we (us) ).

2. Paul told the joke to Luisa and ( I (me) ).

3. Mrs. Russo lives near ( (us) we ).

4. Is this orange juice for Maggie and ( he (him) )?

5. The decorations for the party were made by ( (them) they ).

6. I went to the movies, and a tall man sat down right in front of ( I (me) ).

7. Sarah's mother forgot to give the message to ( (her) she ).

8. Frank spotted his best friend and quickly walked toward ( (him) he ).

9. Everybody has gone home except Chris and ( he (him) ).

10. I went to the Grand Canyon last fall and took pictures of ( (it) her ).

**B.** Write the correct object form of the pronoun in parentheses to complete the sentence.

1. I got a long e-mail from ___[her]___ (she).

2. Vassily stood in front of ___[me]___ (I) in the cafeteria line.

3. I have told this story about Mom and ___[them]___ (they) before.

4. We can't leave for the mall without ___[her]___ (she).

5. My brother Carlos loves fixing up his car. Last weekend he bought some new wheel covers for ___[it]___ (it).

6. Lee wants to work on the science project with Rita and ___[me]___ (I).

7. Everyone is in school today except ___[him]___ (he).

8. Here is an apple for ___[you]___ (you).

9. Bea and Ann divided the cookies among the three of ___[us]___ (we).

10. He called on everyone in class except Ryan and ___[her]___ (she).

# 38. Reviewing Object Pronouns

Use a personal pronoun to replace the word(s) in parentheses.
On the line write **DO** if it is used as a direct object or **OP** if it is
used as the object of a preposition.

__[DO]__ 1. Mohandas Karamchand Ghandi was born in 1869 in India.
Britain ruled ____[it]____ (India) at the time.

__[DO]__ 2. It was arranged that he would marry a girl named Kasturba.
Ghandi married ____[her]____ (Kasturba) when he was thirteen
and she was twelve.

__[OP]__ 3. Ghandi became a lawyer. There was work for ____[him]____
(Ghandi) in South Africa. So he went there.

__[DO]__ 4. In South Africa Indians were treated as an inferior race.
Ghandi helped ____[them]____ (the Indians) gain their rights.

__[OP]__ 5. As for the South African authorities, Ghandi responded
to ____[them]____ (the South African authorities) with nonviolence
and civil disobedience.

__[OP]__ 6. Ghandi had read Henry David Thoreau. From ____[him]____
(Thoreau) Ghandi had learned about civil disobedience.

__[DO]__ 7. Indians in India were not happy with British rule.
They wanted ____[it]____ (British rule) to end.

__[DO]__ 8. Ghandi led ____[them]____ (the Indians) through
nonviolent means to independence.

__[DO]__ 9. As he worked for this independence,
Ghandi would fast. He used ____[it]____
(fasting) to show people that they needed
to be nonviolent as they worked for change.

__[OP]__ 10. The Indian people gave a nickname
to ____[him]____ (Ghandi). They called him
"Mahatma," which means "great soul."

Ghandi used only peaceful means to achieve his goals.
Give an example of some peaceful means you can use
to deal with people who think differently than you do.

Pronouns

# 39. Reviewing Subject and Object Pronouns

**A.** Write the use of the underlined pronoun on the line.
Use the key below.

| SUBJECT | SUBJECT COMPLEMENT | DIRECT OBJECT | OBJECT OF PREPOSITION |
|---------|--------------------|--------------|-----------------------|
| S | SC | DO | OP |

__[S]__ 1. Confucius was an important Chinese philosopher.
He was also a political scientist and a teacher.

__[S]__ 2. He was born in 551 B.C.

__[DO]__ 3. Confucius's father died when Confucius was
three years old, and his mother raised him.

__[SC]__ 4. It was she who was also his first teacher.

__[DO]__ 5. China had fallen into disorder. Local warlords ruled it.

__[SC]__ 6. Confucius was disturbed by the country's problems. It was he
who tried to begin reforms to end the disorder.

__[OP]__ 7. For him it was important that people use their learning to help others.

__[OP]__ 8. He developed rules for good conduct and wrote about them.

__[DO]__ 9. Today people still revere Confucius and honor him.

__[S]__ 10. September 28 is his reputed birthday. It is celebrated as
Teachers' Day in Taiwan.

**B.** Complete each sentence with the correct form of the personal pronoun.
Use the form of the pronoun indicated.

1. ____[He]____ was an important Chinese scholar. (third person, singular,
masculine, subject)

2. His philosophy stressed relationships. The most important of ___[them]___ was
between parent and child. (third person, plural, object)

3. Many people heard of Confucius's philosophy. ____[It]____ was adopted by
many of them. (third person, singular, neuter, subject)

4. At his death, he had more than 3,000 followers. Of ___[them]___, seventy-two
were known as his best disciples. (third person, plural, object)

5. Is Confucianism interesting to ____[you]____? (second person, singular, object)

# 40. Using Reflexive and Intensive Pronouns

A **reflexive pronoun** ends in *-self* or *-selves*. A reflexive pronoun often refers to the subject of the sentence.

> Trent sent <u>himself</u> a message.
> Many inventors do not work by <u>themselves</u>.

An **intensive pronoun** ends in *-self* or *-selves*. An intensive pronoun is used for emphasis.

> I <u>myself</u> made the grilled cheese sandwich.

**A.** Underline the reflexive pronouns. Circle the intensive pronouns.

1. Alexander Graham Bell invented the telephone, but he did not do all the work by <u>himself</u>.

2. Bell had the help of Thomas Watson. Watson (himself) built all of the prototype phones from Bell's designs.

3. Bell and Watson did all the testing of the prototypes by <u>themselves</u>.

4. Bell earned <u>himself</u> the title of inventor of the phone with the first voice transmission in 1876.

5. Bell's wife (herself) Mabel Hubbard Bell, was interested in science.

6. She and her husband built <u>themselves</u> a large home in Canada where they could conduct their research.

7. Mabel Bell was deaf, but she set <u>herself</u> very high ambitions.

8. Mabel Bell was very interested in developing airplanes and other flying machines, though she (herself) was never able to fly in one.

9. Alexander Graham Bell (himself) was responsible for new teaching methods and inventions to help the deaf.

10. We should remind <u>ourselves</u> of all the people like Alexander Graham Bell who helped people have better lives.

**B.** Complete each sentence with the correct reflexive pronoun.

1. I cut _____[myself]_____ while I was chopping onions.

2. Cats clean and groom _____[themselves]_____ with their tongues.

3. We bought ____[ourselves]____ some popcorn to eat during the movie.

4. Oscar, you must do the project for the science fair by ____[yourself]____.

5. Marybeth taught ____[herself]____ the rules of chess.

Name_____

# 41. Using Possessive Pronouns

**Possessive pronouns** show possession or ownership.
The possessive pronouns are *mine, ours, yours, his, hers, its,* and *theirs*.

**That history book is <u>mine</u>.  <u>Yours</u> is in your backpack.**

**A.** Underline the possessive pronoun(s) in each sentence.

1. That new skateboard is <u>hers</u>.

2. <u>Ours</u> is much larger, and <u>yours</u> is much smaller.

3. <u>Mine</u> is purple and green.

4. Those two skateboards must be <u>theirs</u>.

5. <u>His</u> is under the bed.

6. I can't find my bat. Please let me use <u>yours</u>.

7. This bat isn't <u>mine</u>. I think it's <u>his</u>.

8. Excuse me. Is this glove <u>yours</u>?

9. I left <u>mine</u> in the gym at school.

10. Luke lost a glove. This glove must be <u>his</u>.

**B.** Write on the line the possessive pronoun related to the personal pronoun.

1. The green pencil is ____[hers]____ (she), and the
   red pencil is ____[mine]____ ( I ).

2. The idea for the project was ____[theirs]____ (they).

3. Please put your bicycle over there beside ____[ours]____ (we).

4. The last house on the street is ____[his]____ (he).

5. No, those apples are not ____[mine]____ (I).

6. Are these books ____[yours]____ (you)?

7. ____[Mine]____ (I) has been missing for a week.

8. Find ____[yours]____ (you) and then find ____[hers]____ (she).

9. The prize-winning project was ____[hers]____ (she).

10. Is this jacket ____[his]____ (he) or ____[hers]____ (she)?

43

# 42. Using Contractions Containing Pronouns

Personal pronouns can be joined with some verbs to form **contractions**.
An apostrophe (') replaces the missing letter or letters in a contraction.

**I'm** writing a report on Morocco.  =  **I am** writing a report on Morocco.
**We've** never visited Morocco.     =  **We have** never visited Morocco.

**A.** Underline the contraction in each item. Write the pronoun and the verb
that make up the contraction in the correct columns.

|  | PRONOUN | VERB |
|---|---|---|
| 1. Morocco is a fascinating country. It's located in northwest Africa. | [It] | [is] |
| 2. The head of the government is a king. He's named Mohamed VI. | [He] | [is] |
| 3. He's been king since 1999. | [He] | [has] |
| 4. Morocco has many mountains. They're the tallest mountains in northern Africa. | [They] | [are] |
| 5. Many Moroccans have moved to large cities. They've created a severe housing crisis in cities such as Casablanca and Fez. | [They] | [have] |
| 6. Morocco was colonized by Spain and France. It's been independent since 1956. | [It] | [has] |
| 7. Moroccans speak French and Arabic. They're mostly employed in agricultural jobs. | [They] | [are] |
| 8. The capital is Rabat. It's a beautiful city located on the Atlantic Ocean. | [It] | [is] |
| 9. I've never been to Morocco. | [I] | [have] |
| 10. But we're going to visit Morocco next year. | [we] | [are] |

**B.** Complete each sentence with the correct contraction.
Use the pronoun and verb at the left.

He is   1. Morocco's ruler is named Mohamed VI. ____[He's]____ the King of Morocco.

It is   2. ____[It's]____ on the Atlantic Ocean and the Mediterranean Sea.

It has   3. ____[It's]____ been ruled by Spain and France.

They are   4. The people are religious. ____[They're]____ mostly Muslims.

I am   5. ____[I'm]____ going to write a report on Morocco for school.

# 43. Using Interrogative Pronouns

An **interrogative pronoun** is used to ask a question.
The interrogative pronouns are *who, whom, which, what,* and *whose.*

> **What** is the name of the spacecraft that flew to Mars?

The interrogative pronoun *who* is used when the pronoun is the subject of a question.

> **Who** was the first person to walk on the moon?

The interrogative pronoun *whom* is used when the pronoun is the object of a verb or of a preposition.

> **Whom** did the Soviet Union send on the first space flight?

**Pronouns**

**A.** Underline the interrogative pronoun in each sentence.
Write whether it refers to a person or a thing.

__[person]__ 1. <u>Who</u> were the first Americans to land on the moon?

__[thing]__ 2. <u>What</u> did the spacecraft use as fuel?

__[person]__ 3. <u>Which</u> of the astronauts walked on the moon first?

__[person]__ 4. <u>Who</u> called the astronauts on the moon?

__[thing]__ 5. <u>What</u> did the astronauts bring back from the moon?

**B.** Complete each sentence with the correct interrogative pronoun—*which, what,* or *whose.*

1. __[Which]__ of the planets did American spacecraft visit first, Mars or Venus?

2. __[What]__ was the nationality of the first person to travel in space?

3. __[Whose]__ was the promise that the United States would explore the moon within a decade?

4. __[What]__ is a cosmonaut?

5. __[Which]__ of these countries was the first to launch a rocket into space, the Soviet Union or the United States?

**C.** Complete each sentence with the correct interrogative pronoun—*who* or *whom.*

1. __[Who]__ is Neil Armstrong?

2. __[Who]__ was the first Russian to travel in space?

3. To __[whom]__ did the astronauts talk from the moon?

4. __[Whom]__ did you write your report about, Neil Armstrong or John Glenn?

5. __[Who]__ was the captain of the latest Discovery flight?

# 44. Identifying Indefinite Pronouns

> An **indefinite pronoun** refers to any or all of a group of persons, places, or things. Among the indefinite pronouns are *anybody, anyone, anything, everybody, everyone, everything, nobody, no one, nothing, somebody, someone, something, both, few, each, either, many, neither, several, all,* and *some.*
>
> **We're studying European nations. <u>Many</u> are on the Mediterranean.**
>
> **<u>Each</u> of the countries on the Mediterranean use it for recreation.**

**A.** Underline the indefinite pronoun(s) in each sentence.

1. Almost <u>everybody</u> in Italy speaks Italian, and almost <u>everyone</u> in Spain speaks Spanish.

2. <u>Both</u> of the countries have religious freedom.

3. <u>Both</u> have many beautiful churches and museums.

4. The people are very friendly. If you get lost, <u>anybody</u> will help you.

5. <u>Someone</u> mentioned that Spain is bigger in area than Italy.

6. Italy and Spain have similarities: <u>Each</u> is located on a peninsula.

7. <u>Neither</u> has low unemployment.

8. <u>Each</u> has a rich cultural heritage.

9. <u>Each</u> has a language that comes from Latin.

10. Do you want to visit <u>either</u> of these countries?

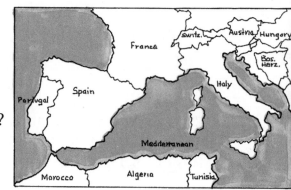

**B.** Complete each sentence with an indefinite pronoun.
**[Possible answers given.]**

1. _____[Both]_____ of the countries are democracies.

2. _____[Neither]_____ is an enemy of the United States.

3. _____[Both]_____ are on the Mediterranean.

4. Do you know _____[anybody]_____ from Spain or Italy?

5. What is the most interesting fact you know about _____[either]_____ of these countries?

# 45. Using Verbs Correctly with Indefinite Pronouns

Many indefinite pronouns are singular and require singular verbs.
They include *anything, everybody, nobody, no one, nothing,* and *somebody.*

SINGULAR    SINGULAR VERB
**Everybody *appreciates* the magnificence of gold.**

Some indefinite pronouns are plural and require plural verbs.
They include *both, few, many, several,* and *some.*

PLURAL                                         PLURAL VERB
**Many of the objects from ancient civilizations *are* of gold or silver.**

**Pronouns**

**A.** An indefinite pronoun in each sentence is underlined. On the line write **S** if it is singular or **P** if it is plural. Circle the correct verb.

___[S]___ 1. Everyone ( (admires) admire ) the beauty of gold and silver.

___[P]___ 2. Both ( has (have) ) been highly valued for hundreds of years.

___[S]___ 3. Neither ( (is) are ) found in great abundance on the earth.

___[P]___ 4. Both of them ( is (are) ) precious metals.

___[S]___ 5. Each ( last (lasts) ) a long time, but silver tends to turn black.

___[S]___ 6. Either of them ( (is) are ) malleable and can be
shaped into different forms easily.

___[P]___ 7. Many of the earth's metals ( (shine) shines ),
and both gold and silver have a luster.

___[P]___ 8. Some of the objects in ancient tombs
( is (are) ) gold jewelry.

___[P]___ 9. Many of the pieces of jewelry ( is (are) ) very beautiful.

___[S]___ 10. Nobody ( (fails) fail ) to admire the magnificent
gold mask of the Egyptian King Tut.

**B.** Complete the sentences with *was* or *were.*

1. Two great gold rushes occurred in United States history.
   Both __[were]__ in the nineteenth century.

2. Each __[was]__ to a different location, California and Alaska.

3. Many of the miners __[were]__ immigrants from Europe and Asia.

4. Everyone __[was]__ interested in getting rich.

5. However, very few __[were]__ lucky enough to find gold.

47

# 46. Avoiding Double Negatives

> The negatives of *something*, *someone*, and *somebody* are *nothing*, *no one*, and *nobody*. However, when a sentence contains a negative word such as *never* or *not*, use *anything*, *anyone*, or *anybody*.
>
> **Kevin could*n't* read <u>anything</u> on the chalkboard.**

**Pronouns**

Circle the correct indefinite pronoun in parentheses.

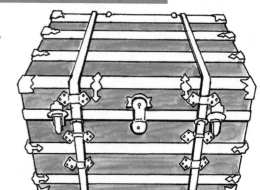

1. Tim didn't find ( nothing (anything) ) in the old trunk in the attic.

2. I'm sorry. There is ( (nothing) anything ) in the mailbox for you today.

3. (Anybody (Nobody) ) spoke about the problem of air pollution.

4. I have never seen ( no one (anyone) ) as tall as Michael Jordan!

5. Sydney broke his arm and can't carry ( (anything) nothing ).

6. ( (Nobody) Anybody ) wants to go out in this terrible rain.

7. I found ( anything (nothing) ) in the parking lot except broken glass.

8. The winner was so excited that she couldn't say ( nothing (anything) ).

9. ( (Nobody) Anybody ) in our class arrived late to school this week.

10. Carmen hasn't eaten ( (anything) nothing ) since breakfast.

11. ( Anybody (Nobody) ) should have been in the park after dark.

12. I didn't tell the secret to ( (anybody) nobody ).

13. Our plan is foolproof! ( (Nothing) Anything) will go wrong.

14. Isn't there ( (anybody) nobody ) who knows a good baseball Web site?

15. The detectives looked for clues, but they couldn't find ( nothing (anything) ).

16. ( (Nobody) Anybody ) could solve the last math problem in the chapter.

17. Bears live near this campground, and so keep all your food in the car. Don't leave ( (anything) nothing ) in your tent.

18. I spent four hours at the mall, but I didn't buy ( (anything) nothing ).

19. There wasn't ( (anything) nothing ) in the refrigerator.

20. Accidents can happen to ( (anyone) no one ).

# 47. Reviewing Pronouns

**A.** Write the person (**1**, **2**, or **3**) and number (**Singular** or **Plural**) of each underlined pronoun in the correct column. Write **S** if it is a subject pronoun or **O** if it is an object pronoun.

| | 1/2/3 | S/P | S/O |
|---|---|---|---|
| 1. We saw a movie titled *Born Free* about Joy and George Adamson. | [1] | [P] | [S] |
| 2. George was a game warden in Kenya. He protected animals. | [3] | [S] | [S] |
| 3. One day a lioness attacked him. | [3] | [S] | [O] |
| 4. He had to shoot her to save his life. | [3] | [S] | [O] |
| 5. He found that she had three cubs, and he took them home. | [3] | [P] | [O] |

**B.** Write the use of each underlined pronoun. Use the key below.

| SUBJECT | SUBJECT COMPLEMENT | DIRECT OBJECT | OBJECT OF PREPOSITION |
|---|---|---|---|
| S | SC | DO | OP |

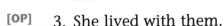

[OP] 1. George and Joy adopted one cub. They gave the name Elsa to her.

[S] 2. She was a beautiful and lively cub.

[OP] 3. She lived with them.

[DO] 4. They raised her in their home.

[SC] 5. The lioness in Joy Adamson's book *Born Free* was she.

**C.** Identify each underlined pronoun. Use the key below.

| REFLEXIVE PRONOUN | POSSESSIVE PRONOUN | INDEFINITE PRONOUN |
|---|---|---|
| R | P | I |

[I] 1. Joy and George loved Elsa, but each knew that there was a problem.

[I] 2. Neither wanted Elsa to live with them forever.

[I] 3. Both wanted Elsa to have a life in the wild.

[R] 4. So Elsa had to learn the skills to survive in the wild by herself.

[P] 5. Joy and George taught Elsa the skills of survival so that a life in the wild could be hers.

CONTINUED

Pronouns

**D.**  Circle the correct personal pronoun.

1. My friends and ( me (I) ) learned a lesson from the movie *Born Free*.

2. Animals have a natural habitat. ( (They) Them ) were born to live in it.

3. Joy raised Elsa. Elsa lived with ( (her) she ) until the lioness was three.

4. Elsa was able to live in the wild. ( (She) Her ) had cubs of her own.

5. Joy wrote about her experiences in the book *Born Free*, and many people have enjoyed reading about ( they (them) ).

**E.**  Circle the correct pronoun.

1. Are you sure there is ( (no one) anyone ) to ( who (whom) ) we can write to learn more about helping wild animals?

2. Doesn't ( no one (anyone) ) know ( (who) whom ) started the Born Free organization?

3. ( (Who) Whom ) hasn't found ( (anything) nothing ) about the group on the Web?

4. Isn't there ( nobody (anyone) ) ( (who) whom ) has observed animals in a natural setting?

5. Can't you tell us ( (anything) nothing ) about the person with ( who (whom) ) you have shared this experience?

## Try It Yourself

Write four sentences about a person you admire. Tell what the person did or does. Explain why you admire him or her. Be sure to use pronouns correctly.

_____

_____

_____

_____

## Check Your Own Work

Choose a selection from your writing portfolio, your journal, a work in progress, an assignment from another subject, or a letter. Revise it, applying the skills you have reviewed. The checklist will help you.

✔ Have you used subject and object pronouns correctly?

✔ Have you formed possessive pronouns correctly?

✔ Have you used interrogative pronouns in your sentences correctly?

✔ Have you avoided double negatives?

Name _____

# 48. Identifying Adjectives

---

An **adjective** describes a noun.

Adjectives       Noun

The <u>huge</u>, <u>colorful</u> *painting* was hanging in the museum entrance.

A **proper adjective** is formed from a proper noun.

<u>Italian</u> artists painted on wet plaster to create fresco paintings.

All other adjectives are **common adjectives**.

This painting has <u>bright</u> colors!

---

**A.** Underline the descriptive adjectives in each sentence.
Write **P** above the proper adjectives and **C** above the common adjectives.

1. Throughout history people have made <u>beautiful</u>[C] colors in <u>different</u>[C] ways.

2. <u>African</u>[P] and <u>European</u>[P] caves display some of the <u>earliest</u>[C] paintings.

3. <u>Early</u>[C] peoples used <u>red</u>[C], <u>yellow</u>[C], and <u>black</u>[C] pigments from the soil.

4. <u>Industrious</u>[C] Egyptians boiled plants to make <u>colorful</u>[C] dyes.

5. <u>Asian</u>[P] peoples made <u>remarkable</u>[C] tools for coloring from clay.

6. <u>European</u>[P] painters in the 1300s made paints from eggs.

7. <u>Modern</u>[C] painters make <u>large</u>[C] paintings in <u>bold</u>[C] colors with <u>acrylic</u>[C] paints.

8. Today crayons from wax and pigment come in <u>numerous</u>[C] colors.

9. <u>Creative</u>[C] artists can use crayons to draw <u>lovely</u>[C] pictures.

10. Look at a <u>big</u>[C] box of crayons, and you might have a <u>difficult</u>[C] choice.

**B.** Write an adjective to describe each noun. **[Answers will vary.]**

1. _____ sunset     6. _____ painting

2. _____ field     7. _____ pizza

3. _____ puppy     8. _____ skateboard

4. _____ boat     9. _____ report

5. _____ artist     10. _____ computer

# 49. Using Descriptive Adjectives

Some common descriptive adjectives tell about age, size, shape, color, or origin. Other descriptive adjectives tell about other qualities.

**In the <u>old</u> basket were <u>large</u>, <u>round</u>, <u>red</u> apples.**

**A.** Put the adjectives in the correct columns.
Then add two of your own in each column.

| circular | large | Danish | new | pink |
|----------|-------|--------|-----|------|
| purple | square | young | tiny | Thai |

| AGE | SIZE | SHAPE | COLOR | ORIGIN |
|-----|------|-------|-------|--------|
| [new] | [large] | [circular] | [pink] | [Danish] |
| [young] | [tiny] | [square] | [purple] | [Thai] |
|  |  |  |  |  |
|  |  |  |  |  |

**B.** Complete the sentences with the correct adjectives. Use the clues in parentheses for help. Use each adjective once.

| bitter | green | healthful | Italian | old |
|--------|-------|-----------|---------|-----|
| orange | popular | round | small | tasty |

1. Zucchini are usually _____[green]_____ (color).

2. They are usually long and _____[round]_____ (shape).

3. Some can be very large, and others can be very _____[small]_____ (size).

4. It is an _____[old]_____ (age) custom to eat fried zucchini in Italy.

5. Large zucchini can be _____[tasty]_____ (quality), but smaller zucchini usually have a better taste.

6. Large zucchini can taste _____[bitter]_____ (quality), which means they are less useful for delicate recipes.

7. *Zucchini* is an _____[Italian]_____ (origin) word that means "little squash."

8. Some people eat the colorful zucchini flowers, which are bright _____[orange]_____ (color) and yellow.

9. Zucchini are _____[healthful]_____ (quality) vegetables; they are a good food for almost everyone's diet.

10. One _____[popular]_____ (quality) recipe for zucchini is zucchini bread; many people make it and like it.

Adjectives

Name_____

# 50. Identifying Adjectives Used as Subject Complements

> An adjective that follows and completes the meaning of a linking verb is called a subject complement. It describes or limits the subject.
>
> SUBJECT (NOUN)        SUBJECT COMPLEMENT (ADJECTIVE)
> **Switzerland   is   <u>mountainous</u>.**

Underline the subject complements.
Circle the nouns they describe.

1. (Switzerland) is <u>small</u>.

2. The (country) is <u>multilingual</u>: People speak German, French, and Italian.

3. (Switzerland) has been <u>neutral</u> during wars.

4. The country's (government) is <u>democratic</u>.

5. (Switzerland) is <u>wealthy</u>.

6. The (people) are <u>industrious</u> and <u>hardworking</u>.

7. Swiss (banks) have long been <u>famous</u> around the world.

8. Industrial (production) is <u>high</u>.

9. Swiss (products) are <u>excellent</u>.

10. Swiss (chocolate) is <u>delicious</u>.

11. Swiss (watches) are <u>famous</u>.

12. The (watches) are very <u>accurate</u>.

13. Many Swiss (watches) also are <u>expensive</u>.

14. Swiss (watchmakers) are <u>meticulous</u> in their work.

15. The (weather) is often <u>rainy</u>.

16. (Winters) are <u>cold</u> and <u>snowy</u>.

17. The (weather) can be <u>foggy</u> in winter too.

18. In winter skiing (conditions) are <u>excellent</u>.

19. During winter months (resorts) are <u>busy</u> with skiers.

20. The Swiss (countryside) is <u>beautiful</u>.

# 51. Understanding the Position of Adjectives

> An adjective usually comes before a noun.
> **Foreign** oil is expensive.
>
> A subject complement follows a linking verb.
> Foreign oil is **expensive**.

**A.** Underline the adjectives used as subject complements. Circle the nouns they describe.

1. The (United States) is <u>rich</u> in natural resources.
2. Its (abundance) of water is <u>helpful</u> to industry.
3. The nation's many (forests) are <u>valuable</u> for their wood.
4. (Coal) is <u>nonrenewable</u>.
5. This (resource) will not be <u>plentiful</u> forever.
6. American (soils) are <u>rich</u> in metals.
7. Certain (metals) are <u>vital</u> to the economy.
8. American iron (mines) are <u>large</u> and <u>productive</u>.
9. America's natural (resources) are <u>important</u>.
10. (People) should be <u>careful</u> to use them wisely.

**B.** Identify the position of each underlined adjective. Use the key below and write your answer above the adjective.

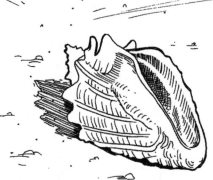

| BEFORE THE NOUN | SUBJECT COMPLEMENT |
|:---:|:---:|
| BN | SC |

1. In summer, the climate of Florida is <sup>[SC]</sup> <u>hot</u>.
2. The weather is often <sup>[SC]</sup> <u>humid</u> too.
3. During these hot months the beaches are <sup>[SC]</sup> <u>crowded</u>.
4. In winter, temperatures are <sup>[SC]</sup> <u>warm</u>.
5. Winter nights are <sup>[SC]</sup> <u>cool</u> and <sup>[SC]</sup> <u>pleasant</u>.
6. Florida has thousands of miles of <sup>[BN]</sup> <u>beautiful</u> beaches.
7. The <sup>[BN]</sup> <u>wonderful</u> beaches and <sup>[BN]</sup> <u>mild</u> climate attract tourists to Florida.
8. Tourism is <sup>[SC]</sup> <u>important</u> to Florida's economy.
9. Florida has <sup>[BN]</sup> <u>fabulous</u> restaurants with <sup>[BN]</sup> <u>excellent</u> seafood.
10. Vacations in Florida can be <sup>[SC]</sup> <u>wonderful</u>.

# 52. Identifying Words Used as Adjectives and Nouns

Some words can be used as nouns and as adjectives.
A noun is a name word. An adjective describes a noun.

| NOUN | ADJECTIVE | NOUN MODIFIED |
|------|-----------|---------------|
| A <u>bat</u> is a mammal. | Large <u>bat</u> | *colonies* are found in caves. |

Above the underlined word in each sentence, write **A** if it is used
as an adjective or **N** if it is used as a noun.

1. Many people are scared of bats, but bats do a great deal of <u>good</u>. [N]

2. For example, bats eat <u>insect</u> pests. [A]

3. In one hour bats can eat about 600 to 1,000 <u>insects</u>. [N]

4. So bats are <u>good</u> for humans because they eliminate harmful insects. [A]

5. They are also good for <u>plants</u>. [N]

6. Many <u>plant</u> species depend on bats for pollination. [A]

7. The bat often lives in a <u>cave</u>. [N]

8. Bats may sleep in large groups hanging from a <u>cave</u> ceiling. [A]

9. Many bats spend the <u>winter</u> months in caves. [A]

10. These bats sleep, or hibernate, during the <u>winter</u>. [N]

11. Bats are primarily <u>night</u> animals. [A]

12. They look for food at <u>night</u> and sleep during the day. [N]

13. Bats use <u>sound</u> to maneuver. [N]

14. Their <u>sound</u> emissions echo back to them, so bats are able to detect objects ahead. [A]

15. The bones in a bat's wing are similar to the bones in a human <u>finger</u>. [N]

16. But the bat's <u>finger</u> bones are very long. [A]

17. Bats' large wings are covered with <u>membranes</u>. [N]

18. The <u>membrane</u> structures of their wings allow bats to scoop insects as they fly. [A]

19. <u>Migration</u> for the winter is characteristic of some bats, as it is for birds. [N]

20. Some bats' <u>migration</u> flights take them from Mexico to the United States. [A]

Adjectives

# 53. Using Articles

> *A, an,* and *the* point out nouns. They are called **articles**.
> *The* is a **definite article**. *A* and *an* are **indefinite articles**.
> The article *an* is used before a vowel sound.
> The article *a* is used before a consonant sound.
>
> **<u>The</u> tourists went to <u>an</u> island for <u>a</u> vacation.**

**A.** Write the correct indefinite article before each word.

1. __[a]__ lieutenant
2. __[an]__ eclipse
3. __[an]__ albatross
4. __[a]__ chauffeur
5. __[a]__ hexagon

6. __[an]__ application
7. __[a]__ dinosaur
8. __[a]__ musician
9. __[an]__ orphan
10. __[a]__ rainbow

11. __[an]__ elephant
12. __[a]__ folktale
13. __[an]__ egg
14. __[an]__ accident
15. __[a]__ cellular phone

**B.** Complete each sentence with definite or indefinite articles as indicated.

1. __[The]__ *(def.)* South Pacific has many islands.

2. It is __[a]__ *(indef.)* part of __[the]__ *(def.)* world that has more water than land.

3. Volcanoes and atolls formed __[the]__ *(def.)* islands of the South Pacific.

4. __[The]__ *(def.)* animals of __[the]__ *(def.)* islands include bats and lizards.

5. Sometimes __[a]__ *(indef.)* typhoon strikes __[the]__ *(def.)* islands.

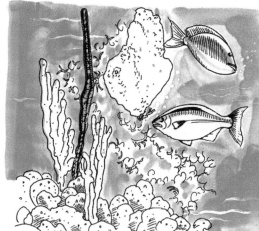

6. __[An]__ *(indef.)* atoll is __[a]__ *(indef.)* coral reef that surrounds __[a]__ *(indef.)* body of water.

7. __[The]__ *(def.)* Great Barrier Reef, __[a]__ *(indef.)* wall of coral, is in Australia.

8. On __[a]__ *(indef.)* reef there is __[an]__ *(indef.)* abundance of wildlife.

9. You might see __[a]__ *(indef.)* shark hiding in __[the]__ *(def.)* shadows.

10. Would you like to visit __[an]__ *(indef.)* island in __[the]__ *(def.)* South Pacific?

Adjectives

# 54. Identifying Numeral Adjectives

A **numeral adjective** indicates an exact number.

Gutenberg was the <u>first</u> person to use moveable type to print a book.

About <u>fifty-one</u> copies of the Bible he printed are known to exist today.

Underline the numeral adjectives in each sentence.
Circle the noun each modifies.

1. Johann Gutenberg lived in Germany during the <u>fifteenth</u> (century.)

2. At that time books were copied by hand, and it sometimes took a scribe <u>two</u> (years) or more to copy a book.

3. Gutenberg, a skilled craftsman and metal worker, spent <u>twenty</u> (years) on his printing experiments.

4. Gutenberg used small pieces of metal, each with <u>one</u> (letter) on it.

5. His type font had <u>290</u> different (characters): letters, punctuation marks, and joined letters required by medieval Latin.

6. He set pages with the type and then printed <u>one</u> (page) at a time on a printing press made from an old wine press.

7. Soon after Gutenberg perfected his press, he had a disagreement with a partner and paid him <u>2,025</u> (guilders,) a great deal of money at that time.

8. Gutenberg printed <u>two</u> (books,) a Bible and another religious work.

9. This Bible had <u>forty-two</u> (lines) of type on each page.

10. Each page had about <u>2,500</u> (characters)—a very large number!

11. <u>Six</u> (typesetters) worked at the same time to set the type for this Bible.

12. This Bible was printed in <u>three</u> (volumes.)

13. It is believed that about <u>200</u> (copies) of the Bible were printed.

14. Gutenberg's system of typesetting was so good that it was used without significant change until the <u>twentieth</u> (century.)

15. His method of printing survived for more than <u>400</u> (years!)

Gutenberg worked patiently for twenty years on his printing experiments. Give an example of a situation in which you have needed patience to achieve your goal.

# 55. Identifying Demonstrative Adjectives

> The **demonstrative adjectives** are *this*, *that*, *these* and *those*.
> *This* and *that* point out one person, place, or thing.
> *These* and *those* point out more than one person, place or thing.
> *This* and *these* name persons, places, or things that are near.
> *That* and *those* name persons, places or things that are far.
>
> **This** rock is a special kind of rock—a fossil.
> **That** rock contains a rare mineral, gold.
> **These** rocks are made of quartz.
> **Those** rocks are nothing but gravel.

**A.** Underline the demonstrative adjective in each sentence.

1. <u>That</u> scientist is a geologist.

2. The formation of <u>this</u> planet is a geologist's field of study.

3. <u>These</u> scientists collect rock samples for study.

4. Fossilized plants and animals help <u>these</u> people reconstruct the past.

5. Fossils are important in <u>this</u> kind of work.

6. Dating <u>those</u> specimens provides useful information to scientists.

7. Many areas of science benefit from <u>this</u> knowledge.

8. <u>That</u> insect was preserved in fossilized tree sap.

9. The name of <u>that</u> fossil is amber.

10. <u>Those</u> plants and animals preserved as fossils lived millions of years ago.

**B.** Complete each sentence with a demonstrative adjective.

1. ___[That]___ *(far)* scientist is a mineralogist.

2. ___[This]___ *(near)* branch of geology studies minerals.

3. ___[Those]___ *(far)* crystals are formed from minerals.

4. ___[This]___ *(near)* pencil contains a mineral—graphite.

5. ___[These]___ *(near)* rocks contain iron, another important mineral.

# 56. Using Those and Them Correctly

Those is used to point out something. Those may be an adjective or a pronoun. Them is always a pronoun. The personal pronoun them can never be used as an adjective.

ADJECTIVE   NOUN MODIFIED          PRONOUN
**Those** *jackets* **are on sale.**    **Those by the escalators are on sale too.**

PERSONAL PRONOUN USED AS AN OBJECT
**I have two new jackets. I bought them at the sale.**

**A.** Circle the correct word in each sentence.

1. ( Those  Them ) flowers bloom in the fall.
2. Do you know ( those  them )  people?
3. Did you see ( those  them ) boys playing soccer?
4. I have known ( those  them ) for years.
5. Who wrote ( those  them ) adventure stories?
6. Cory saw ( those  them ) on television.
7. I have some of ( those  them ) kinds of stamps in my collection.
8. Jane walked with ( those  them ) through the park.
9. The principal congratulated ( those  them ) for their good grades.
10. ( Those  Them ) sentences were not difficult.

**B.** Complete each sentence with *those* or *them*.

1. ____[Those]____ kinds of athletic shoes are expensive.
2. We sent an invitation to ____[them]____.
3. Do you prefer these or ____[those]____?
4. Are you going to continue fixing ____[those]____ two cars?
5. The answers are missing. Can you supply ____[them]____?
6. He walked by his friends without noticing ____[them]____.
7. Are ____[those]____ CDs for sale?
8. My father talked to ____[them]____ about moving to Texas.
9. I am not sure if Mom will like these or ____[those]____.
10. Deciding between ____[them]____ will be difficult.

# 57. Identifying Possessive Adjectives

A **possessive adjective** expresses possession or ownership.
The possessive adjectives are *my, our, your, his, her, its,* and *their.*
   **I got <u>my</u> tetanus shot yesterday.**

**A.** Underline the possessive adjective in each sentence.

1. <u>My</u> report is about vaccines.

2. Vaccines protect <u>our</u> bodies from many diseases.

3. Edward Jenner invented the first vaccine in 1798, and <u>his</u> work had important results.

4. <u>His</u> vaccine protected people against smallpox.

5. He studied a minor disease, cowpox, and noticed <u>its</u> effects on people.

6. When people had had cowpox, <u>their</u> bodies were then able to fight off smallpox.

7. Jenner had an idea: <u>his</u> idea was to inject people with cowpox bacteria.

8. Jenner's experiments were a success in the fight against smallpox, and <u>their</u> results led to the development of other vaccines.

9. Edna told me that she had done <u>her</u> report on vaccines too.

10. We found, however, that <u>our</u> reports focused on different scientists.

**B.** Write the correct form of the possessive adjective on the line.
Use the adjective related to the pronoun in parentheses.

1. People need to do many things to protect ____[their]____ (they) health.

2. We need to make sure that we get all ____[our]____ (we) vaccinations.

3. When you receive a vaccine, it helps ____[your]____ (you) body create antibodies to fight a disease.

4. Sometimes a person's body can create ____[its]____ (it) own antibodies.

5. The vaccines are used to fight very dangerous diseases such as polio, diphtheria, or tetanus. ____[Their]____ (They) effects can cause death.

Adjectives

# 58. Using Possessive Adjectives Correctly

> A possessive adjective expresses possession or ownership.
> A possessive adjective does not have an apostrophe.
>> **Your report is on the fall of the Berlin Wall.**
>
> A **contraction** is formed by joining two words. A contraction has an apostrophe.
>> **You're ( = You are) going to give the report next week.**

**A.** Write **P** over the underlined word if it is a possessive adjective.
Write **C** if it is a contraction.

1. The students studied about the Berlin Wall in <ins>their</ins> [P] social studies class.

2. <ins>Its</ins> [P] fall on November 9, 1989, marked Communism's end in Europe.

3. <ins>It's</ins> [C] been many years since East and West Germany have been reunited.

4. <ins>They're</ins> [C] now a single country.

5. What is <ins>your</ins> [P] opinion about the fall of the Berlin Wall?

**B.** Circle the correct word in parentheses.

1. The people of Poland had many of the same problems as those in East Germany. From 1945 ( (their) they're ) government was Communist.

2. ( (They're) Their ) no longer under Communist rule.

3. ( (Their) They're ) transition to democracy began in 1980.

4. In that year workers formed ( (their) they're ) opposition trade union, Solidarity.

5. ( (Its) It's ) leader was Lech Walesa.

6. Communists opposed the union, and ( (its) it's ) existence was banned.

7. People supported the union, and ( (their) they're ) support kept it alive.

8. In 1989 Poland had an economic crisis. ( It's (Its) ) Communist leaders decided to allow Solidarity to participate in elections.

9. Solidarity won many seats in the Polish congress, and it reformed Poland's economy and gave people back ( (their) they're ) freedoms.

10. The Polish people are glad that ( (they're) their ) free to form their own government.

Name_____

# 59. Identifying Interrogative Adjectives

An **interrogative adjective** is used in asking a question.
The interrogative adjectives are *which*, *what*, and *whose*.

> <u>Which</u> president was from Georgia?
> <u>What</u> flower is the state flower of Ohio?
> <u>Whose</u> portraits are carved into Mount Rushmore?

**A.** Underline the interrogative adjective in each sentence.
Circle the noun it modifies.

1. <u>Which</u> (state) in the United States is the largest?

2. In <u>which</u> (state) was the first U.S. president inaugurated?

3. <u>What</u> (animal) is on the California state flag?

4. <u>Whose</u> (home) in Virginia is named Monticello?

5. <u>Which</u> (group) of islands forms a state?

6. <u>Which</u> (state) is called the Cradle of Presidents because so many presidents have come from there?

7. <u>Whose</u> (residence) is located in Washington, D.C.?

8. <u>What</u> (city) is the capital of Texas?

9. In <u>which</u> (city) is the Statue of Liberty located?

10. In <u>what</u> (state) was the Declaration of Independence approved?

**B.** Complete each sentence with an interrogative adjective.
For some sentences, more than one answer may be correct.

1. [Which/What] state has Raleigh as its capital?

2. In [which/what] state is the Sears Tower located?

3. [Which/What] land did Thomas Jefferson purchase for the United States?

4. In [what] year did Texas become a state?

5. In [whose] honor was Washington, D.C., named?

6. In [which/what] state will you find the Empire State Building?

7. [Whose] portrait is on a dime?

8. [What] year did World War II end?

9. [Which/What] state is the smallest?

10. [Which/What] state do you live in?

# 60. Forming Comparative and Superlative Degrees of Adjectives

> The **positive degree** of an adjective shows a quality of a noun.
>
> **Hydroelectric power, produced from flowing water, isn't very <u>old</u>.**
>
> The **comparative degree** shows a quality of two nouns in greater or lesser degree.
>
> **The steam engine is <u>older</u> than hydroelectric power.**
>
> The **superlative degree** shows a quality of a noun in the greatest or least degree.
>
> **Power from wind and water are among the <u>oldest</u> types of power.**

**A.** Write the comparative and superlative degrees of each adjective.

1. sharp _____[sharper]_____ _____[sharpest]_____

2. heavy _____[heavier]_____ _____[heaviest]_____

3. large _____[larger]_____ _____[largest]_____

4. good _____[better]_____ _____[best]_____

5. cold _____[colder]_____ _____[coldest]_____

6. expensive _____[more expensive]_____ _____[most expensive]_____

7. honest _____[more honest]_____ _____[most honest]_____

8. peaceful _____[more peaceful]_____ _____[most peaceful]_____

9. annoying _____[more annoying]_____ _____[most annoying]_____

10. dangerous _____[more dangerous]_____ _____[most dangerous]_____

**B.** Identify the degree of each underlined adjective. On the line write **C** if it is in the comparative degree or **S** if it is in the superlative degree.

\_\_[S]\_\_ 1. Water is one of our <u>most important</u> natural resources.

\_\_[C]\_\_ 2. Hydroelectric power is <u>cleaner</u> than coal-burning power plants.

\_\_[S]\_\_ 3. Water pollution is one of the country's <u>biggest</u> problems.

\_\_[S]\_\_ 4. Twenty years ago Lake Erie was one of the <u>most polluted</u> lakes in the country.

\_\_[C]\_\_ 5. Today the water in Lake Erie is much <u>purer</u>.

# 61. Using Comparative and Superlative Degrees of Adjectives

> The comparative degree is used when two persons, places, or things are compared.
> **Hurricanes are <u>stronger</u> than tornadoes. They are <u>more destructive</u> too.**
>
> The superlative degree is used when more than two are compared.
> **What was the <u>strongest</u> hurricane in history? Was it <u>most destructive</u>?**

**A.** Circle the correct adjective form in each sentence.

1. Hurricanes are among the ( dangerous (most dangerous) ) storms.

2. Hurricane Andrew, in 1992, was a ( (terrible) more terrible ) hurricane; it caused more than $20 billion in damage.

3. However, it wasn't the ( worse (worst) ) hurricane in history.

4. Which hurricane was the ( (most destructive) more destructive ) in history?

5. A 1926 hurricane was ( (more devastating) most devastating ) than Andrew; it caused twice as much damage.

6. Andrew was not the ( deadly (deadliest) ) hurricane in history either.

7. The ( higher (highest) ) death toll in U.S. history from a hurricane was from one that struck Galveston, Texas, in 1900; more than 8,000 people died.

8. In fact, no other storm has been ( (worse) worst ) than that one.

9. After the storm, the city of Galveston built a ( (large) largest ) seawall.

10. Now the city is ( (safer) safest ) from hurricanes than before.

**B.** Complete each sentence with the correct form of the adjective.

1. The sinking of the *Titanic* was one of the _____[most shocking]_____ (shocking) events in the twentieth century.

2. It is also _____[worse]_____ (bad) than any other tragedy at sea; more than 1,500 people died.

3. When the *Titanic* was built in 1912, it was the _____[biggest]_____ (big) passenger ship in the world.

4. The *Titanic* was also one of the _____[most luxurious]_____ (luxurious) ships.

5. Nowadays ships are _____[safer]_____ (safe) than the *Titanic* because they carry enough lifeboats for everyone aboard.

# 62. Reviewing Adjectives

**A.** On the line write whether each underlined adjective
is common, proper, numeral, demonstrative, possessive, or interrogative.

| | |
|---|---|
| _____[numeral]_____ | 1. E. L. Konigsburg wrote a book about two children who hide in a museum. |
| _____[possessive]_____ | 2. The name of her book is *From the Mixed-up Files of Mrs. Basil E. Frankweiler.* |
| _____[interrogative]_____ | 3. In what city is the Metropolitan Museum of Art? |
| _____[common]_____ | 4. The children have an exciting adventure. |
| _____[possessive]_____ | 5. Their names are Claudia and Jaime. |
| _____[common]_____ | 6. The children see a beautiful sculpture of an angel. |
| _____[demonstrative]_____ | 7. They want to find out about that sculpture. |
| _____[proper]_____ | 8. Was it by the Italian artist Michelangelo? |
| _____[common]_____ | 9. Will they be clever enough to solve the mystery? |
| _____[common]_____ | 10. The story is very suspenseful. |

**B.** Underline the descriptive adjective in each sentence.
Write **BN** above the adjective if it is before a noun.
Write **SC** above the adjective if it is a subject complement.

1. The room in the museum was enormous. [SC]

2. An unusual object attracted our attention. [BN]

3. The object was Egyptian. [SC]

4. It was like a small dollhouse with statues of people inside. [BN]

5. The object was for the use of the dead person in the afterlife. [BN]

**C.** On the line identify the use of each underlined word.
Write **N** if it is a noun or **A** if it is an adjective.

__[A]__ 1. There were many wall hangings.

__[N]__ 2. Scenes of elegantly dressed people on a hunt covered one wall.

__[N]__ 3. Other rooms contained weapons made of bronze.

__[A]__ 4. Bronze tools from an archaeological dig were on display.

__[A]__ 5. I bought a postcard of my favorite works of art.

**D.** Complete each sentence with *this, that, these,* or *those.*

1. ____[This]____ *(near)* room contains arms and armor.

2. ____[That]____ *(far)* chain mail armor differs from
____[this]____ *(near)* plate armor.

3. ____[These]____ *(near)* helmets all have visors, but
____[those]____ *(far)* helmets do not.

4. Look! ____[That]____ *(far)* horse is wearing special armor.

5. Look! Even ____[these]____ *(near)* shoes are in metal.

**E.** Complete each sentence with the correct degree of comparison.

1. What is the ____[most popular]____ *(popular)* exhibit in the museum?

2. The Egyptian statues are ____[older]____ *(old)* than
the Greek statues.

3. Susi thought that the blown glass vases were the ____[prettiest]____
*(pretty)* objects.

4. For Rob the Egyptian room was the ____[best]____ *(good)*
part of the museum.

5. For me the armor was ____[more interesting]____ *(interesting)*
than the sculpture.

## Try It Yourself

Write three sentences about a museum, park, or other place you visited recently.
Describe it. Tell what you found most interesting, the most exciting, and so on.
Be sure to use adjectives correctly.

_____

_____

_____

## Check Your Own Work

Choose a selection from your writing portfolio, your journal, a work in progress,
an assignment from another subject, or a letter. Revise it, applying the skills you
have reviewed. The checklist will help you.

✔ Have you chosen vivid descriptive adjectives?

✔ Have you been careful to use the correct article?

✔ Have you used correct forms for possessive and demonstrative adjectives?

✔ Have you chosen the correct degree of comparison for adjectives?

# 63. Identifying Verbs

A **verb** is a word that is used to express action or state of being.

VERB OF BEING
**The earthquake <u>was</u> very destructive.**

ACTION
**The earthquake <u>destroyed</u> more than 100 major buildings.**

**A.** Write **NS** on the line if the group of words is not a sentence and **S** if the group of words is a sentence. Underline the verb in each sentence.

[S]  1. In 1906 San Francisco <u>experienced</u> a terrible earthquake.

[NS] 2. Early in the morning, at about 5 A.M.

[S]  3. People from Los Angeles to Oregon <u>felt</u> the earth's movement.

[S]  4. The force of the quake <u>toppled</u> many homes and businesses.

[NS] 5. After the earthquake a huge fire.

[S]  6. Broken gas lines <u>caused</u> large fires.

[S]  7. The fire <u>burned</u> much of the central business district.

[NS] 8. Businesses in ruins.

[S]  9. After the quake thousands of people <u>were</u> without homes.

[NS] 10. Years of rebuilding.

**B.** Choose the best verb to complete each sentence.
Use each verb once.

**caused      lost      struck      suffered      was**

1. A major earthquake ____[struck]____ Mexico City in 1985.

2. The center of the earthquake ____[was]____ about 400 miles away from Mexico City.

3. However, the extreme strength of the quake ____[caused]____ considerable damage in the capital city.

4. The city's major buildings ____[suffered]____ damage.

5. More than 10,000 people ____[lost]____ their lives.

# 64. Identifying Verb Phrases

A **verb phrase** is a group of words that does the work of a single verb. Any verb used with a principal verb is called an **auxiliary verb** or **helping verb**. The common auxiliary verbs are the following:

| | | | | | | |
|---|---|---|---|---|---|---|
| be | is | were | had | will | may | could |
| been | are | has | do | shall | can | should |
| am | was | have | did | might | would | must |

**A.** Underline the verb phrase in each sentence.

1. Chimney sweeps have cleaned chimneys for hundreds of years.

2. People should clean their chimneys periodically.

3. Burning wood in a fireplace can leave soot on the chimney walls.

4. After a few years this soot can ignite.

5. A serious fire could be the result.

6. So homeowners must hire a chimney sweep from time to time.

7. Nowadays the number of chimney cleaners has decreased.

8. This is because the number of chimneys has declined.

10. Traditionally chimney sweeps would be small children.

11. They would go into the chimney.

12. Nowadays chimney sweeps are using sophisticated equipment and even video cameras in their jobs.

13. Chimney cleaners should not be afraid of heights.

14. They often must work on steep roofs.

15. Chimney sweeps usually will be very busy before the start of winter.

**B.** Circle the auxiliary verb in each sentence.

1. Nursing (can) be a rewarding profession.

2. Nurses (must) study for at least two years, and some study for four years.

3. Nurses (might) work with people of all ages—from babies to the elderly.

4. In the past nursing (had) been a profession for women.

5. Now many men as well as women (are) entering the profession.

Verbs

# 65. Using Regular and Irregular Verbs

The principal parts of a verb are **present**, **present participle**, **past**, and **past participle**. The present participle is formed by adding -*ing* to the present. The past and the past participle of regular verbs are formed by adding -*ed* or -*d* to the present. The past and the past participle of irregular verbs are not formed by adding -*ed* or -*d* to the present.

| | PRESENT | PRESENT PARTICIPLE | PAST | PAST PARTICIPLE |
|---|---|---|---|---|
| REGULAR | walk | walking | walked | walked |
| IRREGULAR | ride | riding | rode | ridden |

**A.** Write the present participle, past, and past participle of each verb.

| | PRESENT | PRESENT PARTICIPLE | PAST | PAST PARTICIPLE |
|---|---|---|---|---|
| 1. | drift | [drifting] | [drifted] | [drifted] |
| 2. | ring | [ringing] | [rang] | [rung] |
| 3. | rise | [rising] | [rose] | [risen] |
| 4. | stop | [stopping] | [stopped] | [stopped] |
| 5. | choose | [choosing] | [chose] | [chosen] |
| 6. | talk | [talking] | [talked] | [talked] |
| 7. | write | [writing] | [wrote] | [written] |
| 8. | make | [making] | [made] | [made] |
| 9. | go | [going] | [went] | [gone] |
| 10. | fly | [flying] | [flew] | [flown] |

**B.** Complete each sentence with the present participle, past, or the past participle of the verb.

1. The Old North Church has _____[stood]_____ (stand) in Boston for hundreds of years.

2. One cold night before the American Revolution, Paul Revere was _____[waiting]_____ (wait) for a signal.

3. Someone _____[put]_____ (put) lanterns in the steeple to signal the arrival of British troops.

4. Revere _____[rode]_____ (ride) off to warn the people of the British invasion of Massachusetts.

5. While he was riding through the towns and villages, he was _____[shouting]_____ (shout), "The British are coming, the British are coming!"

# 66. Using Lie and Lay; Sit and Set

> The verb *lie (lying, lay, lain)* means "to rest or recline."
>   **Please lie down on the floor for the warm-up exercise.**
>
> The verb *lay (laying, laid, laid)* means "to put in place or position."
>   **He laid the books on the table and sat down to study.**
>
> The verb *sit (sitting, sat, sat)* means "to have or keep a seat."
>   **Please sit down and have some cookies and milk.**
>
> The verb *set (setting, set, set)* means "to place or fix in position."
>   **I set the timer for five minutes.**

**A.** Complete each sentence with the correct form of *lie* or *lay.*

1. Matt, please ____[lay]____ the newspaper on the table.

2. The tourists have ____[lain]____ on the beach all afternoon.

3. Most of Europe ____[lies]____ in the north temperate zone.

4. I ____[laid]____ my glasses somewhere, but I don't remember where.

5. If you are really so sick, I think that you should ____[lie]____ in bed.

6. Mrs. Greene ____[laid]____ out the bride's wedding dress and then helped her get ready.

7. Jeff, where did you ____[lay]____ my coat?

8. My father ____[lay]____ on the couch to watch TV, but he fell asleep.

9. If you start feeling stressed, you should ____[lie]____ quietly, close your eyes, and meditate for a few minutes.

10. The cook ____[laid]____ out a lunch of cold cuts and salads.

**B.** Complete each sentence with the correct form of *sit* or *set.*

1. Please ____[set]____ the buckets in the broom closet.

2. I ____[sit]____ in the front row so that I can take pictures.

3. We ____[sat]____ on the 50-yard-line at the football game last Sunday!

4. I ____[set]____ the two potted palms on either side of the front door. Don't move them.

5. Please ____[set]____ that box on the table and help me move this bed.

Verbs

# 67. Using <u>Rise</u> and <u>Raise</u>; <u>Let</u> and <u>Leave</u>; <u>Teach</u> and <u>Learn</u>

The verb *rise (rising, rose, risen)* means "to ascend."
> **This road <u>rises</u> very steeply, so cars cannot travel very fast.**

The verb *raise (raising, raised, raised)* means "to lift."
> **Please <u>raise</u> your hand if you want to participate.**

The verb *let (letting, let, let)* means "to permit or allow."
> **My dad <u>let</u> me stay up late to watch the movie.**

The verb *leave (leaving, left, left)* means "to abandon or depart."
> **The train <u>left</u> the station right on time.**

The verb *teach (teaching, taught, taught)* means "to give instruction."
> **Carla <u>taught</u> her little brother to play catch.**

The verb *learn (learning, learned, learned)* means "to receive instruction."
> **He <u>learned</u> to swim when he was ten years old.**

**A.** Circle the correct verb in parentheses.

1. ( Rise (Raise) ) the flag quickly and lower it slowly.
2. ( (Let) Leave ) me try to clean the kitchen.
3. Maureen ( (left) let ) for school without her lunch.
4. Please ( (rise) raise ) and say the Pledge of Allegiance.
5. My dad ( (taught) learned ) me to ride a bicycle.

**B.** Complete the sentence with the correct verb in the past tense.

1. Slowly the Loch Ness monster _____[rose]_____ from the murky depths.
2. The ship _____[left]_____ the harbor, on its way to England.
3. My brother _____[taught]_____ me how to play air hockey.
4. The temperature _____[rose]_____ ten degrees this morning.
5. I _____[left]_____ school early today in order to go to the dentist.
6. The bridge keeper _____[raised]_____ the bridge so the boat could sail through.
7. We _____[left]_____ early for the game because traffic was bad.
8. Mr. Lopez _____[taught]_____ art at our school for many years.
9. The president _____[rose]_____ from the chair to begin the State of the Union address.
10. Dad _____[let]_____ me set up the tent.

# 68. Identifying Transitive Verbs

A **transitive verb** expresses an action that passes from a doer to a receiver. Every transitive verb has a receiver of its action. The receiver is the direct object.

DOER                                    RECEIVER
*Eli Whitney* <u>invented</u> the *cotton gin*.

**A.** Underline the transitive verb in each sentence.
Write **D** above the doer and **R** above the receiver.

1. Eli Whitney <u>earned</u> a college degree in 1792.
2. He <u>learned</u> the newest ideas in science and technology.
3. But he <u>needed</u> a job.
4. Phineas Miller <u>helped</u> him.
5. Miller <u>managed</u> a large cotton plantation in Georgia.
6. Whitney <u>studied</u> the operation of the plantation.
7. English companies <u>wanted</u> American cotton.
8. However, these companies <u>did</u> not <u>want</u> the seeds in the cotton.
9. Eli Whitney <u>got</u> an idea for a machine.
10. His machine <u>removed</u> all the seeds quickly and easily.
11. Eli Whitney's work <u>helped</u> the English companies.
12. Cotton planters <u>grew</u> more and more cotton.
13. However, cotton planters <u>did</u> not <u>pay</u> Eli Whitney for his machines.
14. They simply <u>copied</u> his machine.
15. Later, North and South Carolina, Tennessee, and Georgia <u>made</u> payment to him for the invention.

**B.** Choose the best verb to complete each sentence. Write it in the past tense. Use each verb once. Underline the direct object of each verb.

**fit     invent     make     need     put**

1. In 1797 the U.S. government _____[needed]_____ <u>guns</u> for its army.
2. At this time a worker made each part of the gun individually and _____[put]_____ the <u>parts</u> together.
3. Eli Whitney _____[invented]_____ a new <u>system</u>—mass production.
4. Each machine _____[made]_____ only one <u>part</u>.
5. Each part _____[fit]_____ any <u>gun</u>.

Verbs

# 69. Identifying Intransitive Verbs

An **intransitive verb** has no receiver of its action. It does not have a direct object. An intransitive verb may be followed by a prepositional phrase, an adverb, or a subject complement.

**Laura Ingalls Wilder <u>wrote</u> about the American West.**

**A.** Underline the intransitive verb(s) in each sentence.

1. Young Laura Ingalls <u>lived</u> in the Midwest in the late 1800s.

2. Her family <u>farmed</u>.

3. She <u>lived</u> in a house in the woods.

4. Later her family <u>moved</u> from the woods to the prairies farther west.

5. As a young woman Laura <u>married</u>.

6. Later she <u>wrote</u> about pioneer life.

7. She <u>drew</u> on her actual experiences as a girl.

8. Her descriptions of joys and hardships of pioneer life <u>appeal</u> to readers.

9. For example, *A Little House on the Prairie* <u>tells</u> about her trip in a covered wagon from Wisconsin to the West.

10. Laura Ingalls Wilder <u>died</u> in 1957, a well-loved writer.

**B.** Underline the intransitive verb(s) in each sentence.

1. The Amazon River <u>starts</u> in the Peruvian Andes.

2. From the Andes it <u>flows</u> east.

3. It <u>travels</u> across northern Brazil.

4. Finally, after almost 4,000 miles, it <u>arrives</u> at the Atlantic Ocean.

5. The river <u>widens</u> and <u>deepens</u> considerably.

6. In fact, large freighters <u>sail</u> in its waters.

7. The Amazon <u>travels</u> through lush rain forests.

8. Thousands of different creatures <u>live</u> in the Amazon.

9. Catfish, electric eels, and piranhas <u>swim</u> in its waters.

10. Millions of unique plants <u>grow</u> in the rain forest along its shore.

Verbs

# 70. Identifying Verbs That Can Be Transitive or Intransitive

Some verbs can be transitive or intransitive, according to their use in the sentence.

TRANSITIVE VERB     RECEIVER
**Madge ate the *cookies*.**

INTRANSITIVE VERB
**We ate at seven o'clock last night.**

**A.** Underline the verb in each sentence. On the line write **T** if it is transitive or **I** if it is intransitive.

___[I]___ 1. In spring, wildflowers grow along this highway.

___[T]___ 2. We grow flowers in our garden.

___[T]___ 3. The parents hid the presents from their children.

___[I]___ 4. Some animals hide from their predators by their color.

___[I]___ 5. Our class sings every morning.

___[T]___ 6. The class sang the national anthem yesterday.

___[T]___ 7. Jana wrote me an e-mail.

___[I]___ 8. Jana always writes on the computer.

___[T]___ 9. Picasso painted priceless masterpieces.

___[I]___ 10. Picasso painted in different innovative styles.

**B.** Underline the verb in each sentence. On the line write **T** if it is transitive or **I** if it is intransitive. For transitive verbs, circle the receiver (the direct object).

___[T]___ 1. Florence Nightingale, a British woman, founded modern (nursing) in the 1800s.

___[I]___ 2. She rebelled against the idle life of her wealthy family.

___[T]___ 3. She dedicated her (life) to the service of others.

___[I]___ 4. She went with 38 nurses to Turkey during a war there.

___[T]___ 5. They nursed wounded (soldiers).

___[T]___ 6. At first, doctors didn't accept Nightingale's (nurses).

___[I]___ 7. Nightingale's work resulted in improvements in hospitals.

___[I]___ 8. The death rate for ill soldiers fell by two thirds.

___[T]___ 9. She raised (funds) for supplies for soldiers.

___[T]___ 10. She won the (respect) of the British public for her work.

Verbs

# 71. Identifying Linking Verbs

> A **linking verb** links the subject of a sentence with a complement
> (a noun, a pronoun, or an adjective). Verbs of being are linking verbs.
>
> SUBJECT        LINKING VERB   SUBJECT COMPLEMENT
> **John F. Kennedy <u>was</u> the 35th *president* of the United States.**
>
> These verbs can be used as linking verbs: *appear, become, continue, feel, grow, look, remain, seem, smell, sound,* and *taste.*
>
> **He <u>became</u> president in 1961.**

The subject complement in each sentence is underlined. Circle the
linking verb in each sentence. Above each subject complement,
write its part of speech. Use the key below.

NOUN—N          PRONOUN—P          ADJECTIVE—A

1. John F. Kennedy (was) [N] <u>president</u> from 1961 to 1963.

2. He (became) a naval [N] <u>officer</u> in World War II.

3. He (was) very [A] <u>brave</u> during the war.

4. After the war he (became) a [N] <u>politician</u>.

5. He (became) a U.S. [N] <u>representative</u> at the age of 29.

6. Kennedy (became) our chief [N] <u>executive</u> at 44 years of age.

7. He (was) [A] <u>famous</u> for his inspiring speeches.

8. It (was) [P] <u>he</u> who started the Peace Corps.

9. Though a war injury caused him terrible back pain, he always (looked) [A] <u>energetic</u>.

10. He (was) an [N] <u>advocate</u> of civil rights for all Americans.

11. He (was) also [A] <u>interested</u> in space travel.

12. It (was) [P] <u>he</u> who set the goal of landing a spacecraft with astronauts on the moon.

13. He (was) the [N] <u>author</u> of two best-selling books.

14. He (remained) [N] <u>president</u> until his assassination in 1963 in Dallas.

15. Americans (felt) very [A] <u>sad</u> about his death.

John F. Kennedy succeeded despite a serious limitation—severe
back pain from a war injury. Everyone has limitations of one sort
or another. Give an example of a limitation you have and what you
can do to overcome it.

# 72. Identifying Transitive, Intransitive, and Linking Verbs

**A.** Underline the verb in each sentence.
On the line write **T** if it is transitive,
**I** if it is intransitive, or **L** if it is linking.

__[T]__ 1. People throughout the world <u>eat</u> salmon.

__[T]__ 2. Fishers <u>catch</u> millions of salmon each year.

__[L]__ 3. Salmon fishing <u>remains</u> an important industry.

__[I]__ 4. Many salmon <u>live</u> in the north part of the Pacific Ocean.

__[L]__ 5. The Atlantic salmon <u>are</u> native to the North Atlantic Ocean.

__[L]__ 6. Chinook <u>are</u> the largest species of salmon.

__[T]__ 7. Salmon <u>lay</u> their eggs in fresh water.

__[I]__ 8. The eggs <u>hatch</u> in fresh water.

__[I]__ 9. Some salmon <u>travel</u> up rivers during mating season.

__[L]__ 10. Salmon fishing <u>is</u> a popular sport on the Pacific coast.

**B.** Five of these sentences contain linking verbs.
Underline the linking verb and circle the complement.

1. The salmon <u>is</u> (famous) for its long and difficult journeys.

2. At spawning time, salmon swim upstream.

3. They can leap over 10-foot waterfalls.

4. The male salmon <u>is</u> the (protector) of the female during spawning.

5. She deposits her eggs in a stream bed.

6. The male then fertilizes the eggs.

7. The eggs hatch after three or four months.

8. The young salmon <u>are</u> (food) for many predators.

9. The young salmon travel to the ocean and <u>grow</u> (large).

10. Species of salmon sometimes <u>become</u> (rare) because of overfishing.

Name_____

# 73. Identifying Simple Tenses

> The **simple present tense** tells about an action that happens again and again.
> Russia now <u>elects</u> its leader.
>
> The **simple past tense** tells about an action that happened in the past.
> Czars <u>ruled</u> imperial Russia.
>
> The **simple future tense** tells about an action that will happen in the future
> Continuing reforms <u>will help</u> Russia to a better government.

**A.** Underline the verb in each sentence. Write the tense on the line.

____[past]____ 1. Czars <u>had</u> power in Russia until 1917.

____[past]____ 2. In 1917 revolutionaries <u>overthrew</u> the czar.

____[past]____ 3. Communists <u>became</u> dominant in the new government.

____[past]____ 4. Communists <u>controlled</u> Russia for more than 70 years.

____[past]____ 5. In 1991 the Soviet Union <u>ended</u>.

____[past]____ 6. Russia <u>became</u> a republic.

____[present]____ 7. The Communist system no longer <u>rules</u> in Russia.

____[present]____ 8. The Russian people <u>want</u> a democratic government.

____[future]____ 9. <u>Will</u> the Russians <u>build</u> a democratic system?

____[future]____ 10. We <u>will learn</u> the answer in the years to come.

**B.** Complete each sentence with the tense of the verb indicated.

control  1. OPEC, the Organization of Petroleum Exporting Countries, ____[controls]____ the oil production of many countries. *(present)*

join  2. In the past many important oil-producing countries ____[joined]____ the organization. *(past)*

meet  3. Representatives from each of the member countries ____[meet]____ from time to time to discuss oil production. *(present)*

discuss  4. They ____[discuss]____ the levels of oil production. *(present)*

decide  5. Sometimes they ____[decide]____ to lower production. *(present)*

make  6. That ____[will make]____ oil prices increase. *(future)*

cut  7. For example, in the 1970s OPEC ____[cut]____ production. *(past)*

go  8. As a result, gas prices in the United States ____[went]____ up. *(past)*

be  9. There ____[were]____ long lines of cars at the gas pumps. *(past)*

increase  10. ____[Will]____ oil prices ____[increase]____ again? *(future)*

# 74. Identifying the Progressive Tenses

The progressive tenses are formed with the present participle and a form of *be*.
The **present progressive tense** tells about something that is happening right now.

**The children <u>are reciting</u> the nursery rhymes now.**

The **past progressive tense** tells about something that was happening in the past.

**While the children <u>were sitting</u> in a circle, they <u>were listening</u> to the rhymes.**

**A.** Underline the verb in the progressive tense in each sentence.
On the line write **present** if it is in the present progressive tense
or **past** if it is in the past progressive tense.

_____[present]_____ 1. Mrs. Johnson <u>is reading</u> nursery rhymes to the children in preschool.

_____[present]_____ 2. The children <u>are listening</u> intently.

_____[present]_____ 3. They <u>are enjoying</u> the rhymes.

_____[past]_____ 4. When I <u>was growing</u> up, I liked to listen to nursery rhymes too.

_____[past]_____ 5. Sometimes while the teacher <u>was reading</u>, I would recite the words with her.

**B.** Complete each sentence with the correct tense of the verb at the left.

go   1. While Jack and Jill _____[were going]_____ up the hill,
     they were carrying an empty pail. *(past progressive)*

grow  2. Mary, Mary, Quite Contrary _____[is growing]_____
      silver bells in her garden. *(present progressive)*

sit   3. While Humpty Dumpty _____[was sitting]_____
      on the wall, he had a great fall. *(past progressive)*

try   4. All the king's horses and all the king's men _____[were trying]_____
      to put him together again. *(past progressive)*

eat   5. Little Miss Muffett _____[was eating]_____ curds and whey
      while she was sitting on the tuffet. *(past progressive)*

fall  6. According to the old rhyme, London Bridge _____[is falling]_____ down.
      *(present progressive)*

laugh 7. The little boy _____[is laughing]_____ when the cow jumps over the moon.
      *(present progressive)*

sit   8. Little Jack Horner _____[was sitting]_____ in the corner when he was
      eating a pie. *(past progressive)*

get   9. Mother Hubbard _____[was getting]_____ her dog a bone. *(past progressive)*

fly   10. Look! Four and twenty blackbirds _____[are flying]_____ out of the pie!
      *(present progressive)*

# 75. Identifying the Perfect Tenses

> The perfect tenses are formed with the past participle and a form of *have*.
> The **present perfect tense** tells about an action that happened at some indefinite time or an action that started in the past and continues into the present time.
>
> **Marge <u>has made</u> a delicious chocolate cake.**
>
> The **past perfect tense** tells about a past action that was completed before another past action started.
>
> **Homer <u>had eaten</u> three slices before we ate any cake.**

**A.** Underline the verb in the perfect tense in each sentence. On the line write **present** if it is in the present perfect tense or **past** if it is in the past perfect tense.

___[present]___ 1. My mother's family <u>has had</u> a family reunion for many years.

___[past]___ 2. My mother's great-grandfather <u>had started</u> the tradition long before I was born.

___[present]___ 3. My family <u>has gone</u> to the reunion for many years.

___[present]___ 4. We <u>have had</u> a lot of fun every year!

___[present]___ 5. The reunions <u>have been</u> at the local picnic grounds for the last five years.

___[present]___ 6. Cousin Ona <u>has won</u> the sack race so many times that this year I was determined to win.

___[past]___ 7. But this year no one <u>had remembered</u> that the picnic grounds needed to be reserved.

___[past]___ 8. By the time we arrived, other people <u>had taken</u> our spot.

___[past]___ 9. After everyone from our family <u>had arrived</u>, we decided to have the picnic in our back yard.

___[past]___ 10. Aunt Joan <u>had prepared</u> seven quarts of potato salad because she expected a huge crowd.

**B.** Complete each sentence with the correct tense of the verb at the left.

ask  1. Many eager fans ___[have asked]___ the famous movie star for her autograph. *(present perfect)*

try  2. She ___[has tried]___ to avoid them. *(present perfect)*

avoid  3. She ___[has avoided]___ leaving her hotel room. *(present perfect)*

gather  4. Anxiously, the fans ___[had gathered]___ outside her hotel as afternoon approached. *(past perfect)*

hope  5. They ___[had hoped]___ to get her autograph before she left for the Academy Awards ceremony. *(past perfect)*

# 76. Using the Perfect Tenses

Complete each sentence with the indicated tense.

sing 1. Our school's chorus _____[has sung]_____ on TV. *(present perfect)*

sing 2. It _____[had sung]_____ the same song in a concert held last month. *(past perfect)*

choose 3. We _____[have chosen]_____ the date for the picnic. *(present perfect)*

choose 4. We _____[had chosen]_____ the same picnic grove we used two years ago. *(past perfect)*

do 5. Floods _____[had done]_____ damage to the town before this year's record flood nearly submerged it. *(past perfect)*

do 6. This year's flood _____[has done]_____ damage to the entire downtown area. *(present perfect)*

finish 7. I ___[have]___ not ___[finished]___ all my homework yet. *(present perfect)*

finish 8. I _____[had finished]_____ my science project before I started my math assignment. *(past perfect)*

ride 9. I ___[have]___ never ___[ridden]___ the new roller coaster at Adventure Park. *(present perfect)*

ride 10. Once, after I _____[had ridden]_____ a roller coaster three times in a row, I got sick. *(past perfect)*

eat 11. Allison ___[had]___ not ___[eaten]___ sushi before she tasted it this week. *(past perfect)*

eat 12. Allison _____[has eaten]_____ sushi two times already this week! She really likes it! *(present perfect)*

take 13. My brother _____[has taken]_____ several piano lessons, and he can play several songs. *(present perfect)*

take 14. My brother ___[had]___ never ___[taken]___ a music lesson before he attended the concert. *(past perfect)*

travel 15. My friends _____[have traveled]_____ in a helicopter several times. *(present perfect)*

travel 16. They ___[had]___ not ___[traveled]___ in one until they received free tickets. *(past perfect)*

see 17. I ___[had]___ never ___[seen]___ a live shark before I went to the aquarium yesterday. *(past perfect)*

see 18. Now I _____[have seen]_____ both very large and very small sharks. *(present perfect)*

break 19. The students _____[have broken]_____ three beakers in the lab. *(present perfect)*

break 20. Before they dropped the beakers today, they ___[had]___ never ___[broken]___ a single one. *(past perfect)*

Name_____

# 77. Reviewing Tenses

Complete each sentence with the indicated tense of the verb in parentheses.

interest 1. The planet Mars _____[has interested]_____ humans for thousands of years. *(present perfect)*

be 2. Mars _____[is]_____ Earth's neighbor and the seventh-largest planet in the solar system. *(present)*

find 3. In the 1800s people thought that scientists _____[had found]_____ canals on Mars and that this offered proof of life on Mars. *(past perfect)*

see 4. But what the scientists _____[had]_____ _____[seen]_____ were channels, not dug-out canals that people thought were there. *(past perfect)*

write 5. Long before humans sent out spacecraft, science fiction writers _____[were writing]_____ about life on Mars. *(past progressive)*

write 6. In the 1890s H. G. Wells _____[wrote]_____ a book about an invasion of Earth by creatures from Mars called *The War of the Worlds. (past)*

invade 7. In Ray Bradbury's series of stories *The Martian Chronicles,* inhabitants from Earth _____[were invading]_____ Mars. *(past progressive)*

send 8. Since the 1960s Russians, Americans, and Japanese _____[have]_____ _____[sent]_____ spacecraft to explore Mars. *(present perfect)*

pass 9. In 1965 the U.S. spacecraft *Mariner 4* _____[passed]_____ within 9,920 kilometers of the planet's surface. *(past)*

take 10. It _____[took]_____ 22 close-up photos that showed a cratered surface. *(past)*

conduct 11. A lander from the U.S. *Viking 1* _____[conducted]_____ experiments on Mars soil in 1976. *(past)*

conduct 12. Currently the United States _____[is conducting]_____ a series of probes of Mars with the *Odyssey* spacecraft. *(present progressive)*

bring 13. One _____[will bring]_____ back soil from Mars. *(future)*

wonder 14. And people still _____[are wondering]_____ about the possibility of life on Mars. *(present progressive)*

find 15. _____[Will]_____ these spacecraft _____[find]_____ any life on Mars? *(future)*

Verbs

81

# 78. Using Correct Subject-Verb Agreement

> A subject and a verb always agree.
> With all verbs except *be*, the third person singular of the simple present tense end in *-s* or *-es*.
>
> **A senator <u>serves</u> for six years.**
>
> A plural verb does not end in *-s* or *-es*.
>
> **Two senators <u>serve</u> in Congress from each state.**

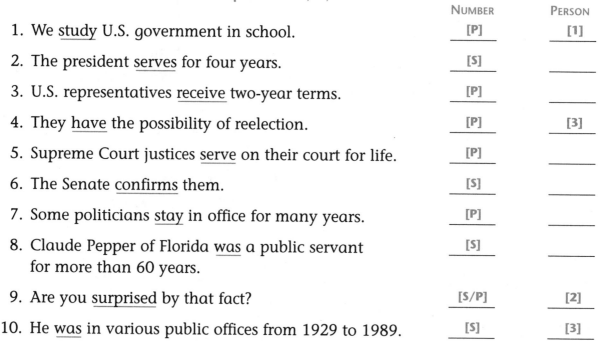

**A.** Underline the verb in each sentence. In the first column write **S** if it is singular or **P** if it is plural. If the subject is a pronoun, in the second column write the person—**1**, **2**, **3**.

|  | NUMBER | PERSON |
|---|---|---|
| 1. We <u>study</u> U.S. government in school. | [P] | [1] |
| 2. The president <u>serves</u> for four years. | [S] | |
| 3. U.S. representatives <u>receive</u> two-year terms. | [P] | |
| 4. They <u>have</u> the possibility of reelection. | [P] | [3] |
| 5. Supreme Court justices <u>serve</u> on their court for life. | [P] | |
| 6. The Senate <u>confirms</u> them. | [S] | |
| 7. Some politicians <u>stay</u> in office for many years. | [P] | |
| 8. Claude Pepper of Florida <u>was</u> a public servant for more than 60 years. | [S] | |
| 9. Are you <u>surprised</u> by that fact? | [S/P] | [2] |
| 10. He <u>was</u> in various public offices from 1929 to 1989. | [S] | [3] |

**B.** If the underlined noun is singular, make it plural. If it is plural, make it singular. Change the verb to agree with the new subject. Write your answers on the lines.

|  | SUBJECT | VERB |
|---|---|---|
| 1. A <u>president</u> takes on many responsibilities. | [presidents] | [take] |
| 2. The <u>presidents</u> hold the executive power. | [president] | [holds] |
| 3. A <u>senator</u> meets with voters. | [senators] | [meet] |
| 4. <u>Members</u> of the House meet with voters. | [member] | [meets] |
| 5. A <u>citizen</u> needs to express opinions. | [citizens] | [need] |

**Verbs**

Name_____

# 79. Using Singular and Plural Subjects; There Is and There Are

When a sentence starts with *there* plus a form of *be*, the subject comes after the verb. The form of *be* must agree with the subject.

**There <u>was</u> an English *colony* in Massachusetts in the 1600s.**
**There <u>were</u> several *children* on board the *Mayflower*.**

**A.** Underline the subject in each sentence.
Circle the correct verb in parentheses.

1. Among the early <u>settlers</u> ( was (were) ) Pilgrims from England.

2. <u>Plymouth</u> ((was) were ) the site of the first permanent settlement of Europeans in New England.

3. Nowadays this old <u>town</u> ((is) are ) a tourist attraction.

4. Many <u>visitors</u> ((come) comes ) to see the town.

5. These <u>tourists</u> ((see) sees ) Plymouth Plantation, a reconstruction of the original settlement.

6. The old <u>houses</u> ( is (are) ) also popular attractions.

7. However, this historic <u>place</u> ((has) have ) more than a tourist-based economy.

8. <u>Boatyards</u> ((line) lines ) the shore.

9. <u>Fishing</u> ((was) were ) important during much of Plymouth's past.

10. Many fishing <u>boats</u> ((continue) continues ) to dock in Plymouth's port.

**B.** Circle the correct verb in parentheses.

1. There ( was (were) ) more than 100 Pilgrims on the *Mayflower*.

2. The Pilgrims arrived in Plymouth in December. There ( was (were) ) many problems for them at first.

3. There ((was) were ) no place to live. They had to clear the land and build a fort.

4. There ((was) were ) very little food that winter.

5. There ((is) are ) a replica of the *Mayflower* in Plymouth Harbor today.

6. There ( is (are) ) many things to see and do in Plymouth today.

7. There ( is (are) ) many restored colonial houses.

8. There ((is) are ) also a large state forest nearby.

9. There ((is) are ) a monument to the Pilgrims in the center of Plymouth.

10. There ( is (are) ) several museums, including a wax museum.

Verbs

# 80. Using Doesn't and Don't; You as the Subject

If the subject of the sentence is in the third person singular, use *doesn't*.
If the subject of the sentence is in the third person plural, use *don't*.
If the subject of the sentence is in the first or second person, use *don't*
whether the subject is singular or plural.

| | |
|---|---|
| THIRD PERSON SINGULAR | ***She* doesn't get up early.** |
| THIRD PERSON PLURAL | ***They* don't get up early.** |
| SECOND PERSON SINGULAR OR PLURAL | ***You* don't get up early.** |

Use you *are* or you *were* whether the subject is singular or plural.

**You are late today, Jennifer.**
**You are late today, Jennifer and Carla.**

**A.** Complete each sentence with *doesn't* or *don't*.

1. A pine tree _____[doesn't]_____ shed its needles in winter.

2. A pine tree's needles _____[don't]_____ get brown either.

3. An evergreen tree _____[doesn't]_____ lose its color in winter.

4. Most other trees in winter in northern climates
   _____[don't]_____ keep their leaves.

5. When a tree loses its leaves in fall, it _____[doesn't]_____ die.

6. The tree just _____[doesn't]_____ produce new leaves until spring.

7. However, all trees will die if they _____[don't]_____ get water.

8. If it _____[doesn't]_____ rain much, even a pine tree may turn brown.

9. During a drought, trees will die if people _____[don't]_____ water them.

10. We _____[don't]_____ need to water the tree in the yard this summer
    because we have had plenty of rain.

**B.** Circle the correct verb in parentheses.

1. ( Is (Are) ) you going on a field trip today with your class?

2. You ( is (are) ) the best speller in class.

3. Sally and Nancy, ( is (are) ) you going to wear your jackets?

4. Jim, ( was (were) ) you in the library this afternoon?

5. ( (Were) Was ) you at the game yesterday?

Verbs

# 81. Using Correct Agreement with Compound Subjects Connected by <u>And</u>

> Compound subjects are connected by *and*. They usually require a plural verb.
> **England *and* France <u>were</u> allies in World War I.**

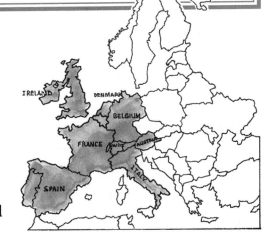

**A.** Circle the correct verb in parentheses.

1. Germany and Austria-Hungary ( was (were) ) allies in World War I.

2. Germany and France ( was (were) ) enemies in World Wars I and II.

3. World War I and World War II ( was (were) ) so terrible that the countries of Europe realized they needed to work together.

4. Austria, Germany, England, and France ( is (are) ) all allies now.

5. Belgium, France, West Germany, Italy, Luxembourg, and the Netherlands ( was (were) ) the first members of the original European organization in 1958.

6. England and Spain ( was (were) ) admitted later.

7. England, France, Germany, and Italy now ( (work) works ) together in the European Union.

8. Political cooperation and economic unity ( (represent) represents ) basic goals of the European Union.

9. People and goods ( (move) moves ) freely among the countries in the Union.

10. As a result, war and conflict ( has (have) ) become less likely in Europe.

**B.** Circle the correct verb. Add words to complete the sentences. **[Answers will vary.]**

1. World War I and World War II ( was (were) ) _____.

2. England, France, and Germany ( has (have) ) _____.

3. The European Union and the United States ( is (are) ) _____.

4. Belgium and Luxembourg ( has (have) ) _____.

5. France and Germany ( (share) shares ) _____.

Verbs

# 82. Using Correct Verb Agreement with Indefinite Pronouns

The indefinite pronouns *each, either, neither, anyone, no one, anybody, nobody, everyone, everybody, someone,* and *somebody* are always singular and require singular verbs.

**Each** of the students <u>has</u> a responsibility in the classroom.
**Someone** <u>unlocks</u> the school doors at 8.
Nearly **everyone** <u>arrives</u> by 8:45.

**Verbs**

**A.** Complete each sentence with the correct form of the verb at the left in the present tense.

know 1. Everyone ____[knows]____ our school's routine.

say 2. Everybody ____[says]____ the Pledge of Allegiance every day.

raise 3. Someone ____[raises]____ the flag each morning.

sing 4. Everyone ____[sings]____ the national anthem every morning, too.

take 5. Each of the teachers ____[takes]____ attendance.

lower 6. At the end of the day someone ____[lowers]____ the flag.

follow 7. Each of the classes ____[follows]____ an end-of-the-day routine too.

erase 8. Somebody in each class ____[erases]____ the boards.

go 9. Everybody except the principal and assistant principal ____[goes]____ home at 3:30.

leave 10. Neither of them ____[leaves]____ until five o'clock.

**B.** Write about the routine at your school. Circle the correct verb. Add words to complete the sentences. **[Answers will vary.]**

1. Almost everybody ( (arrives) arrive ) _____.

2. Hardly anybody ( come (comes) ) _____.

3. Somebody ( clean (cleans) ) _____.

4. Everyone ( (is) are ) _____.

5. Everybody ( sing (sings) ) _____.

# 83. Using Correct Verb Agreement with Special Nouns

> Nouns such as *deer, fish, sheep, swine, trout, salmon, cod, moose, corps,* and certain proper nouns such as *Portuguese, Chinese, Swiss,* and *Iroquois* have the same form in the singular and the plural. The sense of the sentence indicates whether the subject is singular or plural.

**A.** Underline the subject in each sentence. Above the subject, write **S** if it is singular and **P** if it is plural. Circle the correct verb in parentheses.

1. A famous [S] <u>Sioux</u> ( (was) were ) Crazy Horse, who led his tribe in a war against the United States government.

2. Red [P] <u>salmon</u> ( is (are) ) caught in Puget Sound.

3. The [P] <u>Iroquois</u> ( was (were) ) allies of the British in the wars of the 1700s.

4. Look! A [S] <u>deer</u> ( (is) are ) eating grass in the back yard.

5. The [P] <u>Spanish</u> ( lives (live) ) on the Iberian Peninsula.

6. The [P] <u>Sioux</u> ( (belong) belongs ) to the group called the Plains Indians.

7. [P] <u>Trout</u> ( (live) lives ) mainly in fresh water.

8. A [S] <u>moose</u> ( (is) are ) a member of the deer family.

9. [P] <u>Reindeer</u> ( was (were) ) brought from Siberia to Alaska.

10. Some [P] <u>sheep</u> ( is (are) ) waiting to be sheared.

11. [P] <u>Deer</u> ( is (are) ) timid by nature.

12. These [P] <u>fish</u> ( is (are) ) such a lovely orange-red color.

13. A [S] <u>Portuguese</u>, Bartolomeu Dias, ( (is) are ) remembered for his explorations.

14. The [P] <u>Chinese</u> ( (inhabit) inhabits ) the world's most populous country.

15. A small [S] <u>goldfish</u> ( (was) were ) raised by the class in this fish tank.

**B.** Circle the correct verb. Add words to complete the sentence. **[Answers will vary.]**

1. This deer ( live (lives) ) _____.

2. A Sioux ( (is) are ) _____.

3. The Chinese ( (live) lives ) _____.

4. That small sheep ( (has) have ) _____.

5. Trout ( (swim) swims ) _____.

Verbs

# 84. Reviewing Correct Subject-Verb Agreement

**A.** Circle the correct verb in parentheses.

1. African Americans ( (celebrate) celebrates ) a holiday in December.

2. ( (Are) Is ) you familiar with the holiday?

3. Its name ( (is) are ) Kwanzaa.

4. There ( is (are) ) seven days of celebration.

5. Each of the days ( (is) are ) devoted to a different principle, such as unity, creativity, and faith.

6. On December 31 everybody ( (participates) participate ) in a feast.

7. There ( is (are) ) special plays and speeches at the feast.

8. Children ( doesn't (don't) ) receive gifts until January 1.

9. The Swahili ( (celebrate) celebrates ) a similar harvest holiday, as do other African peoples.

10. The feast ( (doesn't) don't ) have a long history in this country; it began in 1966.

**B.** Complete each sentence with the correct form of the verb at the left in the present tense.

house 1. This building ___[houses]___ stray dogs and cats.

want 2. Each of the children ___[wants]___ to use the computer.

be 3. There ___[are]___ ten tomatoes on the counter.

be 4. ___[Are]___ you ready for the class play?

be 5. The flowers and vase ___[are]___ on the coffee table.

be 6. Everyone ___[is]___ going to get an ice-cream sundae.

have 7. The French ___[have]___ many great paintings in museums.

be 8. Look! There ___[is]___ a shooting star!

need 9. This fish ___[needs]___ some food in its fish tank.

crow 10. A rooster ___[crows]___ every morning.

# 85. Reviewing Verbs

**A.** Underline the verb or verb phrase in each sentence.
If there is an auxiliary verb, write it on the line.

_____ 1. Michelangelo <u>lived</u> in Italy.

[can] 2. You <u>can see</u> one of his famous works, the *Pietà*, in Rome.

[will] 3. You <u>will feel</u> amazement at the sculpture's power.

[has] 4. The sculpture <u>has traveled</u> to the United States.

[could] 5. People <u>could see</u> it in New York at a World's Fair in the 1960s.

**B.** Write the forms for each verb.

|  | PRESENT PARTICIPLE | PAST | PAST PARTICIPLE |
|---|---|---|---|
| 1. sing | [singing] | [sang] | [sung] |
| 2. walk | [walking] | [walked] | [walked] |
| 3. grow | [growing] | [grew] | [grown] |
| 4. drop | [dropping] | [dropped] | [dropped] |
| 5. put | [putting] | [put] | [put] |

**C.** Underline the verb in each sentence. On the line
write **T** if the verb is transitive or **I** if it is intransitive.

[T] 1. Michelangelo <u>carved</u> magnificent statues.

[I] 2. He also <u>painted</u>.

[T] 3. He <u>painted</u> the ceiling of the Sistine Chapel in Rome.

[T] 4. Michelangelo <u>depicted</u> the story of creation and other
Bible stories on the ceiling of the Sistine Chapel.

[I] 5. He <u>died</u> in 1564.

**D.** Circle the linking verb in each sentence. On the line
write **N** if the underlined subject complement is a noun
or **A** if it is an adjective.

[A] 1. Michelangelo (became) <u>famous</u> during his lifetime.

[N] 2. He (was) a highly respected <u>artist</u>.

[N] 3. The dome of St. Peter's in Rome (is) a <u>design</u> of his.

[A] 4. Many people (feel) <u>awed</u> by its magnificence.

[N] 5. Michelangelo (was) also a wonderful <u>architect</u>.

CONTINUED

Verbs

Name_____

**E.** What is the tense of the underlined verb in each sentence?
Write *present, past, future, present progressive, past progressive,*
*present perfect,* or *past perfect* on the line.

_____[present perfect]_____ 1. People <u>have known</u> about peanuts
since ancient times.

_____[present]_____ 2. A peanut <u>is</u> not actually a nut.

_____[present]_____ 3. Peanuts <u>belong</u> to the legume—bean—family.

_____[past progressive]_____ 4. Peanuts <u>were growing</u> in the Americas
long before the arrival of Europeans.

_____[past perfect]_____ 5. They <u>had grown</u> in South America before
they came to North America.

_____[past]_____ 6. Peanuts first <u>grew</u> in the South.

_____[past]_____ 7. George Washington Carver <u>created</u>
more than 300 products with peanuts—
including printer's ink and soap.

_____[present perfect]_____ 8. People <u>have eaten</u> peanuts as snacks
since the 1860s.

_____[present perfect]_____ 9. Peanut butter <u>has teamed</u> with jelly in
sandwiches since the 1920s.

_____[present progressive]_____ 10. Nowadays people <u>are eating</u> many
peanut products.

## Try It Yourself
Write three sentences about a painting or sculpture you like. Describe
the work of art. Tell why you like it. Be sure to use verbs correctly.

_____

_____

_____

## Check Your Own Work
Choose a selection from your writing portfolio, your journal, a work in progress, an
assignment from another subject, or a letter. Revise it, applying the skills you have
reviewed. The checklist will help you.

✔ Have you used correct forms of the irregular and regular verbs?

✔ Have you been careful when you used any of the troublesome verbs?

✔ Have you correctly formed verbs in the different tenses?

✔ Do all of your subjects and verbs agree in number?

Verbs

# 86. Identifying Adverbs of Time

An **adverb** is a word that modifies a verb, an adjective, or another adverb. **Adverbs of time** answer the question *when* or *how often* and usually modify verbs.

> **She has already read a few books of myths.** (modifies *has read*)
> **She often reads Aesop's fables.** (modifies *reads*)

Adverbs of time include *again, already, always, before, early, ever, finally, first, frequently, immediately, later, never, now, often, once, recently, seldom, sometimes, soon, still, today,* and *usually.*

**A.** Circle the adverb of time in each sentence. Underline the verb it modifies.

1. People <u>have</u> (always) <u>been</u> curious about the natural world.

2. Ancient myths—or stories—(often) <u>attempted</u> to explain things in nature.

3. Ancient people, including the Greeks, (frequently) <u>created</u> stories about the origins of the world and the things in it.

4. (Later) the ancient Romans <u>borrowed</u> myths from the Greeks.

5. The main characters of these myths <u>were</u> (usually) gods or heroes.

6. <u>Have</u> you (ever) <u>seen</u> a horse with wings?

7. Well, the mythical horse Pegasus (sometimes) <u>flew</u> through the air.

8. The names of the planets (still) <u>reflect</u> the influence of mythology.

9. (First), the telling of myths <u>was</u> part of an oral tradition.

10. (Finally), poets such as Homer <u>wrote</u> the myths down.

**B.** Circle the correct adverb of time.

1. We have ( (already) ever ) begun our study of classical art.

2. Many classical sculptures are ( (now) often ) in the British Museum.

3. The sculpture of ancient Greece has ( (seldom) yesterday ) been equaled.

4. Visitors to Greece can see examples of classical statues ( (today) ever ).

5. ( (Once) Always ) I saw a picture of the Venus de Milo.
   This ancient sculpture has no arms!

6. People ( (often) early ) wonder what the arms would look like.

7. Another famous statue, the Winged Victory, ( (now) never ) lacks its head.

8. People ( (usually) seldom ) think that classical statues were white.

9. Scholars believe that the ancients ( (always) before ) painted the statues.

10. When the statues were found, the paint had ( (already) never ) worn off.

# 87. Identifying Adverbs of Place

**Adverbs of place** answer the question *where* and usually modify verbs.

**Please don't play catch <u>inside</u>.**

**The supermarket is on the next block. You can walk <u>there</u>.**

Adverbs of place include *above, away, back, below, down, far, forward, here, in, inside, outside, there, up,* and *within.*

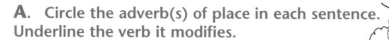

**A.** Circle the adverb(s) of place in each sentence. Underline the verb it modifies.

1. The eagle <u>soared</u> (upward) in its flight.

2. The little boy's dog <u>ran</u> (away).

3. Bright stars <u>twinkled</u> (overhead).

4. <u>List</u> all your suggestions (below).

5. Orioles <u>build</u> nests (high) in the trees.

6. Beautiful paper lanterns <u>hung</u> (here) and (there) among the trees.

7. Because of the blizzard, we <u>didn't go</u> (outside) for two days.

8. <u>Place</u> the table (here), please.

9. The boy <u>went</u> (inside) for his boots.

10. Please <u>look</u> (up) when you finish the exercise.

**B.** Circle the correct adverb of place in each sentence.

1. Our neighbors have just moved ( (away) downward ).

2. Please look ( inside (outside) ) and see if it is raining.

3. You've gone the wrong way. You need to walk ( (back) here ) two blocks and then turn right.

4. We looked ( away (around) ) for the missing books.

5. The batter swung too ( (low) down ) and missed the ball. He was out!

6. The two new polar bears are over ( up (there) ).

7. The kittens should not be left alone ( (outside) below ).

8. Please sign your name ( (here) forward ), Ms. Bergen.

9. Don't look ( (down) far ) or you'll get dizzy.

10. We were so cold that we had to go ( (inside) far ).

# 88. Identifying Adverbs of Manner

**Adverbs of manner** answer the question *how* or *in what manner*. They usually modify verbs.

> **She learned math <u>quickly</u>.**

Some adverbs of manner are *bravely, carefully, cheerfully, clearly, gracefully, swiftly, steadily, quickly,* and *softly*.

Many, but not all, adverbs of manner end in *–ly*. Three common exceptions are *fast, well,* and *hard*.

> **She worked <u>hard</u> all afternoon.**

**A.** Write an adverb of manner for each adjective.

1. proud     [proudly]
2. excited     [excitedly]
3. happy     [happily]
4. soft     [softly]
5. intelligent     [intelligently]

6. easy     [easily]
7. beautiful     [beautifully]
8. diligent     [diligently]
9. tireless     [tirelessly]
10. thoughtful     [thoughtfully]

**B.** Circle the adverb(s) of manner in each sentence. Underline the verb it modifies.

1. Barbara McClintock, a scientist, <u>worked</u> (carefully) and (determinedly).
2. She (deservedly) <u>won</u> a Nobel Prize for Medicine in 1983 for her own individual work.
3. An intelligent woman, she (quickly) <u>earned</u> a Ph.D.—in two years.
4. Genetics interested her, and she <u>studied</u> cells (intently).
5. She (painstakingly) <u>examined</u> the genetic structure of corn.
6. She <u>worked</u> (hard) in her laboratory.
7. In 1931 she (unexpectedly) <u>discovered</u> the role of chromosomes as the basis of genetics.
8. Many scientists (foolishly) <u>rejected</u> her ideas.
9. She (patiently) <u>rechecked</u> her research.
10. Other scientists' discoveries later (clearly) <u>supported</u> her work.

Barbara McClintock continued to work even when others said that she was wrong. She showed that she had tremendous confidence in herself. Name one or two ways you can show that you have confidence in yourself.

# 89. Identifying Adverbs of Degree

**Adverbs of degree** answer the question *how much* or *how little*.
They may modify verbs, adjectives, or other adverbs.

> He wrote <u>well</u>. (modifies *wrote*, a verb)
> The story is <u>rather</u> interesting. (modifies *interesting*, an adjective)
> He traveled <u>rather</u> extensively. (modifies *extensively*, an adverb)

Adverbs of degree include *almost, greatly, merely, quite, too, really, extremely, rather, very, much, hardly, fully, scarcely, barely,* and *partly.*

Circle the adverb of degree in each sentence.
Underline the word it modifies.
Over the word modified write **V** for verb,
**Adj** for adjective, or **Adv** for adverb.

1. Spain is (very) [Adj] <u>famous</u> for the exploration of North and South America.

2. Spaniards did not discover America; they (merely) [V] <u>explored</u> it.

3. The civilizations in the Americas were (quite) [Adj] <u>sophisticated</u>.

4. Some Spanish explorers and writers have left (really) [Adj] <u>interesting</u> accounts of the civilizations in the Americas.

5. Spain's exploration in other parts of the world is (hardly) [V] <u>discussed</u>.

6. However, Ruy Gonzalez de Clavijo (rather) [Adv] <u>daringly</u> traveled to the Middle East in the fifteenth century.

7. Gonzalez, a Spanish diplomat, went from Spain to Turkey and Iran in 1403, a time when travel was (rather) [Adj] <u>difficult</u>.

8. He met Tamburlaine, an Islamic king, who was (very) [Adj] <u>powerful</u>.

9. Tamburlaine had built an (extremely) [Adj] <u>large</u> empire in Asia.

10. He was a fierce fighter and <u>was</u> (greatly) [V] <u>feared</u> by his enemies.

11. Tamburlaine treated his enemies (rather) [Adv] <u>cruelly</u>.

12. He wanted to make his capital at Samarkand (very) [Adj] <u>beautiful</u>.

13. The mosque there has (very) [Adj] <u>lovely</u> mosaics of turquoise and gold.

14. Gonzalez wrote a (really) [Adj] <u>fascinating</u> account of his trip and Tamburlaine's kingdom.

15. Many people have never heard about this (quite) [Adj] <u>unusual</u> trip.

Adverbs

# 90. Identifying Adverbs of Affirmation and Negation

> Adverbs of affirmation and negation tell whether a statement is true or false.
> The **adverbs of affirmation** include *yes*, *indeed*, and *undoubtedly*.
>> **You know who Annie Oakley is undoubtedly.**
>
> The **adverbs of negation** include *no*, *not*, and *never*.
>> **No, I have never read about her.**

**A.** Underline the adverb(s) of affirmation and negation.
Above each write **A** if it indicates affirmation or **N** if it indicates negation.

1. [A] Yes, Annie Oakley was an American sharpshooter and entertainer.

2. [A] Indeed, she could shoot dimes tossed into the air.

3. She was a star of "Buffalo Bill" Cody's Wild West show, and her
   sharpshooting feats [N] never failed to surprise audiences.

4. [N] No, her real name was [N] not Annie Oakley; it was Phoebe Ann Moses.

5. [A] Undoubtedly, she was an amazing person.

**B.** Underline the adverb in each sentence. Write on the line what it indicates.
Use the key below.

TIME—T    PLACE—P    MANNER—M    DEGREE—D    AFFIRMATION—A    NEGATION—N

[D] 1. The Northwest Ordinance of 1787 had a very important role in
the history of Ohio, Indiana, Illinois, Michigan, and Wisconsin.

[T] 2. First, the Ordinance organized the distribution of land in the territory.

[P] 3. The land there was divided according to a grid system.

[M] 4. Land was carefully divided into townships—
large squares of six miles on each side.

[T] 5. Next, each township was divided into
individual sections—one mile on each side.

[T] 6. One of these sections was always set aside for schools.

[M] 7. People quickly bought the individual sections.

[M] 8. The Ordinance also carefully specified the procedure
for new states to join the Union.

[T] 9. Finally, the Ordinance granted key civil rights to the residents
of the territory, including freedom of religion.

[A] 10. Indeed, the Northwest Ordinance of 1787 prohibited slavery in the area.

Adverbs

# 91. Forming Comparative and Superlative Degrees of Adverbs

> The **comparative** and **superlative** of most adverbs that end in *-ly* are formed by adding *more* or *most* before the positive.
> The comparative and superlative of adverbs that don't end in *-ly* are formed by adding *-er* or *-est*.
>
> **A computer can do this work <u>more efficiently</u>.**
> **I can work <u>faster</u> if I use a computer to help me.**
>
> Two common exceptions are *well*, whose comparative and superlative are *better* and *best*, and *badly*, whose comparative and superlative are *worse* and *worst*.

**A.** On the lines write the comparative and superlative form of each adverb.

|  | COMPARATIVE | SUPERLATIVE |
|---|---|---|
| 1. early | [earlier] | [earliest] |
| 2. wisely | [more wisely] | [most wisely] |
| 3. badly | [worse] | [worst] |
| 4. fast | [faster] | [fastest] |
| 5. gracefully | [more gracefully] | [most gracefully] |

**B.** On the line write the comparative form of the adverb at the left.

early   1. The day of the field trip we got up _____ [earlier] _____ than usual.

fast   2. Mercury spins on its axis _____ [faster] _____ than Venus.

late   3. Our guests arrived _____ [later] _____ than we expected.

clearly   4. He speaks _____ [more clearly] _____ than he writes.

slowly   5. Please speak _____ [more slowly] _____ .

**C.** On the line write the superlative form of the adverb at the left.

far   1. Andrew threw the Frisbee _____ [farthest] _____ .

clearly   2. Of all the students in our class, Brice talks _____ [most clearly] _____ .

fast   3. Marlene finished the assignment _____ [fastest] _____ .

near   4. Melody is sitting _____ [nearest] _____ to the blackboard.

carefully   5. Of all the bus drivers, Mr. Pulaski drives _____ [most carefully] _____ .

Adverbs

# 92. Using the Comparative and Superlative Degrees of Adverbs

**A.** Circle the correct form of the adverb.

1. The bus left ( (later) latest ) than we expected.

2. Doug cooks ( (more often) most often ) than he used to.

3. Can you walk ( (faster) fastest ) than that?

4. The last surfer rode the waves ( more gracefully (most gracefully) ).

5. The bells rang ( (more loudly) most loudly ) than usual.

6. Please examine this fossil ( more carefully (most carefully) ) of all.

7. Jason cooks ( (worse) worst ) than Allen.

8. Jonathan skated ( (more skillfully) most skillfully ) than Bert.

9. Marty works ( more diligently (most diligently) ) of all the students in class.

10. You are making a lot of noise, Karen and Linda. Please work ( (more quietly) most quietly ).

**B.** Complete each sentence with the correct form of the adverb.

closely    1. We looked ____[more closely]____ at the gems than at the other rock specimens in the exhibit.

easily     2. Of all the math problems in the assignment, I solved this one ____[most easily]____.

well       3. The basketball team played ____[better]____ today than yesterday.

fast       4. Please work a little ____[faster]____.

clearly    5. Kate was selected for the play because she speaks ____[more clearly]____ than Cindy.

violently  6. The volcano erupted ____[more violently]____ than it had in decades.

hard       7. At the end-of-year assembly, Tyrone won the prize for working ____[hard]____ all year.

politely   8. Of all the clerks, Ms. Grimes deals with customers ____[most politely]____.

softly     9. Please play that music ____[more softly]____.

rapid      10. Express mail is delivered ____[more rapidly]____ than regular mail.

# 93. Using Adverbs and Adjectives Correctly

An adjective describes a noun or a pronoun.
An adjective may follow a linking verb.

NOUN DESCRIBED            ADJECTIVE
**That *sound* from the radio isn't very <u>clear</u>.**

An adverb modifies a verb, an adjective, or another adverb.

VERB MODIFIED            ADVERB
**Actors *must say* their lines <u>clearly</u>.**

Circle the correct word in parentheses. Then
write on the line whether the correct word is
used as an **adjective** or an **adverb**.

__[adjective]__ 1. During the Revolution, Tories
were ( (loyal) loyally ) to Britain.

__[adjective]__ 2. The crossing guard always looks
( (cheerful) cheerfully ) in the morning.

__[adverb]__ 3. Rita plays the violin ( good (well) ).

__[adjective]__ 4. The new bus driver seems very ( (capable) capably ).

__[adverb]__ 5. Please move that computer ( careful (carefully) )
so you don't drop it.

__[adverb]__ 6. The child ( forgetful (forgetfully) ) left her toy on the lawn.

__[adverb]__ 7. The teacher explained the math problems very ( good (well) ).

__[adjective]__ 8. The oatmeal tasted ( (delicious) deliciously ).

__[adjective]__ 9. This pink and orange sunset is really ( (beautiful) beautifully ).

__[adjective]__ 10. Marcy is always ( (thoughtful) thoughtfully ) of others.

__[adverb]__ 11. The students worked ( quiet (quietly) ) on their own.

__[adverb]__ 12. Mrs. Lee ( generous (generously) ) donated a million
dollars to charity.

__[adjective]__ 13. The nurses in that hospital are very ( (helpful) helpfully ).

__[adverb]__ 14. The director spoke ( angry (angrily) ) to the cast
during rehearsals.

__[adverb]__ 15. Margie ( polite (politely) ) thanked her grandmother
for the gift.

Adverbs

# 94. Using There and Their; Two, To, and Too

*Their* is an adjective and shows possession.
*There* is an adverb that means "in that place."
*There* is sometimes an introductory word, usually before the verb *be*.

**Orchids are beautiful. Their petals are lovely. *(possessive adjective)***
**Go to the conservatory. You can see orchids there. *(adverb)***
**There are many varieties of orchids. *(introductory word)***

*Two* is a numeral and refers to the number 2.
*Too* is an adverb and has the same meaning as *also* or *more than enough*.
*To* is a preposition and usually indicates motion toward some place or thing.

**Two birds we see in our yard are orioles and robins. *(numeral)***
**Orioles are in the blackbird family, and bobolinks are too. *(adverb)***
**We gave food to the orioles in the birdfeeder. *(preposition)***

**A. Circle the correct word.**

1. ( Their (There) ) are many kinds of orchids in the world.

2. Wild orchids can grow on tree trunks. Look for them ( their (there) ).

3. People love orchids because of ( (their) there ) beautiful colors.

4. Many people grow orchids on ( (their) there ) porches.

5. ( Their (There) ) are many different kinds of wild orchids in Florida.

**B. Circle the correct word.**

1. A rare South American heron flew ( (to) two ) Austin, Texas, in 1997.

2. The bird should have flown south ( (to) too ) Argentina.

3. Early one morning ( (two) too ) bird lovers spotted it on a lake.

4. Excited, they talked ( (to) too ) others in a bird-watchers' club.

5. These people wanted to see the bird ( to (too) ).

6. The bird lovers gave pictures of the bird ( (to) two )
   a local newspaper.

7. The next day more than fifty people were at the lake.
   The poor bird got scared and flew ( (to) too) another
   lake farther from the city.

8. At summer's end, the confused bird flew back ( (to) two ) South America.

9. However, the next summer ( (two) to ) herons came to Austin.

10. The bird had returned and brought a friend ( (too) to).

# 95. Using Negatives; Identifying Words Used as Adjectives and Adverbs

> If a sentence has a negative adverb, such as *not*, avoid using another negative word, such as *no* or *never*. Use a word like *any* or *ever* instead.
>
> ### ***Never* eat any wild mushrooms.**
>
> Some words can be used as an adjective or an adverb. An adjective describes or limits a noun or a pronoun. An adverb modifies a verb, an adjective, or another adverb.
>
> ### **A fast car drove past. *(adjective)***
> ### **Police cars must drive fast in an emergency. *(adverb)***

**A.** Circle the correct word in parentheses.

1. There are things people should ( never ever ) do around the house.
2. Don't plug ( any no ) more than three objects into one outlet.
3. Don't ( ever never ) put a knife in a toaster when it is plugged in.
4. Never put ( any no ) wires under a rug or carpet.
5. ( Never Ever ) touch an electrical wire with wet hands.
6. Don't ( ever never ) put your fingers directly into an electrical outlet.
7. ( No one Anyone ) should use a power tool without wearing safety glasses.
8. Don't leave ( any no ) toys or shoes in the middle of the floor.
9. ( Ever Never ) keep household cleansers within reach of small children.
10. ( Any No ) sharp objects should be where toddlers can find them.

**B.** The underlined words are adverbs or adjectives. Circle all the adverbs.

1. We climbed a high volcano while we were in Hawaii.
2. The hawk soared high in the sky.
3. Su-Lin likes math better than English.
4. Lisa feels better now.
5. The fast train will arrive in New York before midnight.
6. Work fast and we will be finished before lunch.
7. Daily practice is necessary to becoming a top athlete.
8. The newspaper is delivered to our house daily.
9. Drive west four blocks. The hospital is on the left.
10. The west wing of White House has offices.

# 96. Reviewing Adverbs

**A.** Underline the adverb in each sentence.
Write on the line the kind of adverb it is. Use the key below.

| TIME | PLACE | MANNER | DEGREE | AFFIRMATION | NEGATION |
|------|-------|--------|--------|-------------|----------|
| T | P | M | D | A | N |

___[T]___ 1. We saw a great baseball game <u>recently</u>.

___[M]___ 2. Runners from the opposing team were on first and second base, and we waited <u>anxiously</u> for the pitcher to throw the ball.

___[M]___ 3. Our pitcher threw the ball <u>hard</u>.

___[P]___ 4. The batter swung <u>low</u> and missed.

___[M]___ 5. The runner <u>unexpectedly</u> tried to steal third base.

___[N]___ 6. The runner did <u>not</u> make it. The catcher threw the ball to the player at third base, who tagged the runner.

___[M]___ 7. The fans jumped to their feet <u>excitedly</u>.

___[P]___ 8. I jumped <u>up</u> with the others!

___[D]___ 9. The crowd <u>really</u> cheered!

___[A]___ 10. <u>Yes</u>, our team held its lead!

**B.** Circle the correct adverb in parentheses. On the line write **C** if the adverb is comparative or **S** if it is superlative.

___[S]___ 1. Sound travels very quickly. It travels ( faster (fastest) ) of all in solid materials.

___[C]___ 2. Sound travels ( (more slowly) most slowly ) through gases than through solid materials.

___[C]___ 3. Light travels ( (more quickly) most quickly ) than sound.

___[C]___ 4. Light travels ( (better) best ) through transparent solids like clear glass than through translucent solids such as frosted glass.

___[S]___ 5. Light travels through space ( faster (fastest) ).

**C.** Circle the correct word in parentheses. Write on the line whether it is an **adjective** or an **adverb**.

___[adverb]___ 1. Marta looked at the large box ( hopeful (hopefully) ).

___[adjective]___ 2. She was ( (eager) eagerly ) to see the contents.

___[adverb]___ 3. Her mother ( careful (carefully) ) opened the mysterious box.

___[adverb]___ 4. Marta waited ( patient (patiently) ) while she finished opening it and pulled out a present.

___[adjective]___ 5. Marta felt ( (happy) happily ) about the beautiful book her grandmother had sent her.

CONTINUED

Adverbs

**D.** Complete each sentence with *their* or *there*.

1. ___[There]___ are many nice places to visit in California.
2. Redwood National Forest is ___[there]___.
3. ___[There]___ are many huge trees in the park.
4. The trees are very old. No one knows ___[their]___ exact age.
5. ___[Their]___ height often exceeds 300 feet.

**E.** Complete each sentence with *to*, *too*, or *two*.

1. In 1849 many people went ___[to]___ California to look for gold.
2. Some people made fortunes from gold, but people made money in other ways ___[too]___.
3. Levi Strauss made money selling special pants ___[to]___ miners.
4. Strauss's pants had ___[two]___ advantages: they were strong and they were cheap.
5. People called these pants jeans, but they called these pants Levi's ___[too]___.

**F.** Circle the correct word in parentheses.

1. My friends have ( ever (never) ) been to California.
2. Has no one ( (ever) never ) visited a movie studio?
3. We didn't see ( (any) no ) movie stars when we were there.
4. There wasn't ( (any) no ) sight more impressive than the redwoods.
5. We had ( ever (never) ) seen such tall trees before.

## Try It Yourself

Write three sentences about an exciting event that you attended or saw on TV. Be sure to use adverbs correctly.

_____

_____

_____

## Check Your Own Work

Choose a selection from your writing portfolio, your journal, a work in progress, an assignment from another subject, or a letter. Revise it, applying the skills you have reviewed. The checklist will help you.

✔ Have you included appropriate adverbs of time, place, and manner?

✔ Have you used the correct form for adverbs used in comparisons?

✔ Have you used adverb forms, and not adjective forms, where they are needed?

✔ Have you followed the rules for avoiding double negatives?

**Adverbs**

# 97. Identifying Prepositions

A **preposition** is a word that comes before a noun or pronoun. The preposition shows the relation of the noun or pronoun to some other word in a sentence. The noun or pronoun that follows the preposition is called its object.

OBJECT

**Frederick Douglass made many contributions <u>to</u> the *country*.**

Some common prepositions are *in, into, of, on, to, by, for, from, at, after, against, with,* and *without*.

**Circle the prepositions in each sentence.**

1. Frederick Douglass was one (of) the most important human rights leaders (of) the 19th century.

2. He was born (into) slavery (in) Maryland (with) the name Frederick Bailey.

3. Shortly (after) his birth, his owners separated him (from) his slave mother.

4. His mother moved 20 miles away, a long distance (in) those days.

5. When he was seven or eight, his owner had him work (for) the Auld family (in) Baltimore.

6. (At) that time he learned reading (from) Mrs. Auld.

7. When children (in) the neighborhood finished their books, they gave them (to) young Frederick.

8. (Against) all odds Frederick continued teaching himself.

9. When he was older, Frederick escaped (on) a train, and he lived (in) New York, now a free person.

10. He changed his name (to) Douglass.

11. Douglass began speaking (against) slavery.

12. He became a consultant (to) President Abraham Lincoln.

13. He helped convince Lincoln that slaves should be freed (if) they fought (in) the Civil War (against) the South.

14. (After) the war, Douglass pressed (for) full civil rights (for) freed slaves.

15. Frederick Douglass became the first African-American diplomat when he was appointed U.S. ambassador (to) Haiti.

**Frederick Douglass worked hard to educate himself and then used his education to help others. Give an example of how can you use your education to help others.**

Name_____

# 98. Identifying Prepositional Phrases

A preposition and the noun or pronoun that follows it are separate words, but they do the work of a single modifier. This group of related words is called a **phrase**. Because it is introduced by a preposition, this phrase is called a **prepositional phrase**.

**The Mississippi River is the largest river <u>in the United States</u>.**

**A.** Underline the prepositional phrase(s) in each sentence. Circle each preposition.

1. The Mississippi River starts (in) Minnesota (near) the Canadian border.
2. It flows (toward) the south.
3. The river becomes navigable south (of) St. Paul, Minnesota.
4. Two major tributaries, the Missouri and the Ohio Rivers, flow (into) it.
5. The Missouri River joins the Mississippi River (at) St. Louis.
6. The river is joined (by) the Ohio River, and then it becomes huge.
7. (In) many places, the river is a mile and a half (from) shore (to) shore.
8. This river is one (of) the busiest commercial waterways (in) the world.
9. The river floods (in) spring, which causes damage (to) cities (near) the river.
10. The Mississippi empties (into) the Gulf (of) Mexico (through) a huge delta.

**B.** Write a prepositional phrase about the Mississippi River for each preposition. Circle the object of the preposition.

1. through _____ [Answers will vary.] _____
2. near _____
3. from _____
4. over _____
5. in _____

**C.** Write sentences using each prepositional phrase from Part B.

1. _____ [Sentences will vary.] _____
2. _____
3. _____
4. _____
5. _____

Prepositions, Conjunctions, Interjections

104

Name_____

# 99. Using At and To; Between and Among

At shows presence in. *To* shows motion toward.

> **Ed and Bert are <u>at</u> the museum. They're going <u>to</u> the gold exhibit.**

Use *between* to speak of two persons, places, or things.
Use *among* to speak of more than two.

> **There is much trade <u>between</u> the United States and Canada.**
> **There is trade <u>among</u> the United States, Canada, and Mexico.**

**A.** Complete each sentence with *at* or *to*.

1. Our class took a trip __[to]__ New York.

2. We spent the morning __[at]__ the
   United Nations headquarters.

3. We sailed __[to]__ the Statue of Liberty.

4. We stood __[at]__ the foot of the statue.

5. Then we walked __[to]__ the top.

6. After that we went __[to]__ Ellis Island.

7. Many immigrants __[to]__ the United States arrived at Ellis Island.

8. We also went __[to]__ the Metropolitan Museum of Art.

9. We saw many important paintings __[at]__ the museum.

10. We also saw the animals __[at]__ the zoo in Central Park.

**B.** Complete each sentence with *between* or *among*.

1. The United Nations (UN) works for peace _____[among]_____ all the nations
   of the world.

2. The treaty written by the North Atlantic Treaty Organization (NATO)
   is an agreement _____[among]_____ various Western powers.

3. It was signed during the cold war _____[between]_____ the East and the West.

4. Trade _____[between]_____ the United States and Mexico has been increasing.

5. The United States wants to increase trade _____[among]_____ all countries
   of North and South America.

# 100. Using Beside and Besides; In and Into

> *Beside* means "at the side of" or "next to."
> *Besides* means "in addition to" or "except."
>
> **The driver stood <u>beside</u> his car.**
>
> **Seven students are in the tennis class <u>besides</u> me.**
> Use *in* to show location within something.
> Use *into* to show motion toward a place or a change of location.
>
> **Rabbits live <u>in</u> burrows.**
>
> **If a rabbit is surprised, it will run <u>into</u> its burrow.**

**A.  Circle the correct preposition.**

1. The jockey stood ( (beside) besides ) her horse, Holly's Hope.
2. There are seven horses in the race ( (besides) beside ) Holly's Hope.
3. What kind of ice cream do you like ( (besides) beside ) strawberry?
4. I don't like any flavor ( beside (besides) ) mint.
5. Our class planted a tree ( (beside) besides ) the school building.
6. ( (Besides) Beside ) the tree, we also hope to buy and plant a rose bush.
7. ( Beside (Besides) ) the gorilla, the snow leopard is an endangered species.
8. The naturalist sat right ( (beside) besides ) the gorilla in the wild.
9. There are three students absent today ( (besides) beside ) Jeanette.
10. The girl who sits ( besides (beside) ) me is a new student from Mexico.

**B.  Circle the correct preposition.**

1. The diver put on a wetsuit and jumped ( in (into) ) the water.
2. The diver went right ( (into) in ) a large underwater coral reef.
3. The diver saw many unusual creatures ( into (in) ) the reef.
4. Many of the reef's inhabitants live ( (in) into ) colorful shells.
5. Small fish swim ( (into) in ) crevices in the reef if a predator is near.
6. They will hide ( (in) into ) the crevices until the danger goes away.
7. The diver shined a light ( (into) in ) a crevice.
8. He saw a number of fish ( into (in) ) the darkness.
9. A small shark sometimes swims ( in (into) ) a coral reef.
10. All the other fish hide ( (in) into ) safe places until the shark goes away.

Name_____

# 101. Identifying Words Used as Prepositions and Adverbs

A preposition shows a relationship between its object and some other word in the sentence. An adverb tells *how*, *when*, or *where*. Many words can be used as either prepositions or adverbs.

PREPOSITION

**Help is available to the flood victims <u>through</u> the Red Cross.**

ADVERB

**Because of the flood, trains could not get <u>through</u>.**

**A.** On the line write **P** if the underlined word is a preposition or **A** if it is an adverb.

___[A]___ 1. Please open the door and come <u>in</u>.

___[P]___ 2. A large fire was burning <u>in</u> the fireplace.

___[P]___ 3. The coffee shop <u>across</u> the street opens at 6 A.M.

___[A]___ 4. Our teacher always gets his ideas <u>across</u> clearly.

___[A]___ 5. Rex, my dog, is always <u>near</u> when I'm home.

___[P]___ 6. Rex's bed is <u>near</u> the back door.

___[A]___ 7. Please put that box <u>down</u> in the kitchen.

___[P]___ 8. The kitchen is <u>down</u> those stairs.

___[P]___ 9. There was helium <u>inside</u> the balloon.

___[A]___ 10. On cold days I stay <u>inside</u> and work on my computer.

**B.** Write sentences using each adverb or prepositional phrase.

1. outside *(adverb)* _____ **[Sentences will vary.]** _____

2. outside the door _____

3. up *(adverb)* _____

4. up the stairs _____

5. past *(adverb)* _____

6. past the house _____

7. through the door _____

8. through *(adverb)* _____

9. in *(adverb)* _____

10. in the garden _____

Prepositions, Conjunctions, Interjections

107

Name_____

# 102. Identifying Conjunctions Used to Connect Words

> A **conjunction** is a word used to connect words, phrases, or clauses in a sentence.
> The **coordinating conjunctions** are used to connect similar words or groups of words; they connect words that have the same use in a sentence.
> These words may be nouns, verbs, adjectives, or adverbs.
> They are *and, but, or, nor, yet, for,* and *so.*
>
> > Canadians can watch U.S. TV *shows* or Canadian TV *shows.* (nouns)
> > Canada is *large* but relatively *sparse* in population. (adjectives)
> > The Canadian hockey team skated *quickly* and *agilely.* (adverbs)

**A.** Circle the conjunction in each sentence. Underline the words it connects.

1. Canada's most important industries are mining and manufacturing.

2. Lakes and streams are abundant in northwestern Canada.

3. Manitoba and Ontario are two Canadian provinces.

4. In parts of Canada you can speak English or French.

5. For many Canadians the first language is not English but French.

6. People travel between Canada and the United States without a passport.

7. The Great Lakes are in Canada and the United States.

8. Queen Elizabeth of England is the head of state and monarch of Canada.

9. The preferred term for the Native Americans of northern Canada is not Eskimo but Inuit.

10. Fishing and tourism are important industries in Canada.

**B.** Complete each sentence with words connected by the conjunction.
[Answers will vary.]

1. _____ and _____ are states that border my state.

2. My favorite subjects in school are _____ and _____.

3. Today I feel _____ but _____.

4. Tonight I will watch _____ or _____ on TV.

5. My favorite foods are _____ and _____.

Prepositions, Conjunctions, Interjections

# 103. Identifying Conjunctions Used to Connect Prepositional Phrases

> Coordinating conjunctions can connect prepositional phrases.
> **Many different holidays are celebrated *with fireworks* and *with parades*.**

**A.** Circle the conjunction in each sentence. Underline the phrases it connects.

1. On July 14 Bastille Day is celebrated <u>in France</u> (and) <u>in French territories</u>.
2. France's independence day is celebrated <u>with dancing</u> (and) <u>with fireworks</u>.
3. Soldiers <u>on foot</u> (and) <u>in military vehicles</u> parade down Paris streets.
4. Dragon Boat Day is a fun day <u>in China</u> (and) <u>in Chinese communities</u>.
5. People race long boats <u>with dragon head fronts</u> (and) <u>with twisting dragon tails</u>.
6. Cinco de Mayo is celebrated <u>in Mexico</u> (and) <u>by Mexican-American communities</u>.
7. It marks Mexico's victory <u>over the French</u> (and) <u>over the French colonial ambitions</u>.
8. Street fairs <u>with parades</u> (and) <u>with folk dancing</u> are held throughout Mexico.
9. Citizenship Day on September 17 was a replacement <u>for Constitution Day</u> (and) <u>for I Am American Day</u>.
10. It gives honor both <u>to native U.S. citizens</u> (and) <u>to naturalized citizens</u>.
11. On September 28 Confucius's birthday is celebrated <u>in China</u> (and) <u>by Confucius's followers</u>.
12. In some places there are lectures <u>on Confucius's philosophy</u> (and) <u>about his life</u>.
13. On Earth Day, in April, people learn <u>about the environment</u> (and) <u>about pollution</u>.
14. People ride <u>to work</u> (or) <u>to school</u> on bicycles.
15. People think <u>about conservation</u> (and) <u>about recycling</u>.

**B.** Write sentences with the prepositional phrases.

1. with music and with dances

    [Sentences will vary.] _____

2. on the street and in the home

_____

3. in Mexico and in the United States

_____

4. during the afternoon and at night

_____

5. with special foods and with gifts

_____

Name_____

# 104. Identifying Conjunctions Used to Connect Clauses

> Coordinating conjunctions can connect independent clauses.
> An **independent clause** is a group of words that has a subject and a predicate and expresses a complete thought. When a conjunction joins independent clauses, use a comma before the conjunction.
>
> *Most crocodiles live in fresh water*, **but** *some crocodiles live in salt water.*

**A.** Circle the conjunction in each sentence. Underline the clauses it connects.

1. Crocodiles are in a group called crocodilians, (and) alligators belong to the same group.

2. Crocodiles have a protruding tooth, (but) alligators do not have one.

3. Alligators have a broad snout, (but) the snout of a crocodile is narrow.

4. Both animals live in the southeastern part of the United States, (and) they are found in swamps and on river banks.

5. Alligators rest during the day, (and) they hunt at night.

6. They may float below the surface, (or) they may rest in a hole on a bank.

7. Crocodiles eat small aquatic animals, (but) they do sometimes attack larger mammals.

8. Alligators do not usually attack humans except in self-defense, (but) large crocodiles have been known to try to eat humans.

9. Alligators were in danger of extinction, (but) now laws protect them.

10. Alligators are out of danger, (and) their numbers have increased.

**B.** Combine each pair of sentences with an appropriate coordinating conjunction.

1. Alligators live in the Southeast. They don't live in the West.

   [Alligators live in the Southeast, but they don't live in the West.]

2. Alligators were hunted for their skins. The skins were used for clothing.

   [Alligators were hunted for their skins, and the skins were used for clothing.]

3. People tried to save the alligators. Their efforts were successful.

   [People tried to save the alligators, and their efforts were successful.]

4. Laws were passed to limit hunting. These laws were effective.

   [Laws were passed to limit hunting, and these laws were effective.]

5. Some people are afraid of alligators. Alligators seldom attack humans.

   [Some people are afraid of alligators, but alligators seldom attack humans.]

Name_____

# 105. Reviewing Conjunctions

Underline the conjunction in each sentence.
Write on the line whether it connects **words**, **phrases**, or **clauses**.

___[words]___ 1. Edward played and sang.

___[phrases]___ 2. Seeds are sown by hand or by machine.

___[clauses]___ 3. You can take the bus, or you can take the train.

___[words]___ 4. The coldest months are January and February.

___[words]___ 5. Lewis and Clark explored western Louisiana.

___[clauses]___ 6. Gloria bought the candy, but Ken ate it.

___[words]___ 7. My mother speaks English and Spanish fluently.

___[phrases]___ 8. The fox ran under the hedge and into the field.

___[words]___ 9. Maryland and Virginia gave land for the U.S. capital.

___[phrases]___ 10. These houses are for sale or for rent.

___[clauses]___ 11. The morning was rainy, but the afternoon was sunny.

___[words]___ 12. Broccoli and cauliflower are delicious.

___[clauses]___ 13. He ate one sundae, and he ordered another one.

___[phrases]___ 14. The jelly is on the table or in the refrigerator.

___[words]___ 15. Some airlines offer music and movies.

___[clauses]___ 16. Kate made a skirt, and Elaine knitted a sweater.

___[words]___ 17. Norway and Sweden are alike in several ways.

___[clauses]___ 18. Peter shook the tree, and an apple fell to the ground.

___[clauses]___ 19. Take the expressway, and you will arrive sooner.

___[words]___ 20. Skiing and snowboarding are winter sports.

Prepositions, Conjunctions, Interjections

# 106. Identifying Interjections

An **interjection** is a word that expresses a strong or sudden emotion. Interjections may express happiness, disgust, pain, agreement, impatience, surprise, sadness, amazement, and so on.

**<u>Oh, no!</u> The baby spilled a whole box of cereal on the floor!**
**<u>Wow!</u> Tito Lopez is performing in our town this week.**

Underline the interjections. Write on the line what feeling or emotion each interjection expresses.

___[Answers will vary.]___ 1. <u>Look!</u> It's a family of bears.

_____ 2. He likes to eat fried pickles. <u>Gross!</u>

_____ 3. <u>Oh, no!</u> The test is today.

_____ 4. <u>Hush!</u> The president is about to speak!

_____ 5. <u>Good!</u> That was a great answer!

_____ 6. Today is Friday! <u>Hooray!</u>

_____ 7. You have a new cell phone? <u>Great!</u>

_____ 8. <u>Oops!</u> I dropped my sandwich.

_____ 9. <u>Ouch!</u> That plate is very hot.

_____ 10. <u>Oh!</u> So that's how you turn on this computer.

_____ 11. <u>Wow!</u> That shirt is really expensive.

_____ 12. <u>Oh, dear!</u> It's raining cats and dogs, and I forgot my umbrella again.

_____ 13. We're having pizza for lunch. <u>Yum!</u>

_____ 14. <u>Yes!</u> Our team has won the city championship.

_____ 15. <u>Wonderful!</u> We're going to the mall this afternoon.

_____ 16. <u>Hey!</u> Put that back.

_____ 17. <u>No!</u> You can't be serious.

_____ 18. Pavarotti sings on this CD. <u>Excellent!</u> I love his voice.

_____ 19. <u>Oh, my!</u> That sure costs a lot of money.

_____ 20. You'll be receiving a scholarship. <u>How great!</u>

Name_____

# 107. Reviewing Prepositions, Conjunctions, and Interjections

**A.** Underline the prepositional phrases in each sentence.
Circle each preposition.

1. (In) many Asian countries, people eat (with) chopsticks.

2. Chopsticks are two long thin pieces (of) wood.

3. Some chopsticks are made (from) plastic, porcelain, ivory, or jade.

4. (During) the Middle Ages, some aristocrats used silver chopsticks.

5. They believed silver turned color if it came (into) contact (with) poison.

6. The Chinese have been using chopsticks (for) 5,000 years.

7. Long ago people cooked food (in) large pots, and they gradually cut it (into) smaller and smaller pieces.

8. They removed the food (from) the pots (with) twigs.

9. Gradually the twigs were replaced (by) chopsticks.

10. It's possible that Confucius influenced the development (of) chopsticks because he thought that knives were too violent (for) use (at) the table.

**B.** Circle the correct word in parentheses.

1. Are there any fish ( beside (besides) ) goldfish in this tank?

2. Please plant the tree ( (beside) besides ) the fence.

3. Many fans went ( at (to) ) the rock concert last night.

4. What do you have ( into (in) ) your shoe?

5. Can you find your size ( between (among) ) all of the shoes on the racks?

6. It didn't take long for Andrea to feel ( to (at) ) home with her relatives.

7. The cowboy drove the horses ( in (into) ) the corral.

8. Dan wanted to sit ( (beside) besides ) his friends at the party.

9. Mrs. Martin is ( into (in) ) the office.

10. Who won the game ( (between) among ) Chicago and Pittsburgh?

CONTINUED

**C.** Circle the conjunction in each sentence.
Underline the elements it connects. Write on the line whether
the coordinating conjunctions connect **words**, **phrases**, or **clauses**.

_____[words]_____ 1. Do you want <u>cereal</u> (or) <u>toast</u> for breakfast?

_____[words]_____ 2. A good diet includes plenty of <u>fruits</u> (and) <u>vegetables</u>.

_____[phrases]_____ 3. Do you want your pie <u>with ice cream</u> (or) <u>with whipped cream</u>?

_____[clauses]_____ 4. <u>People should eat a balanced diet,</u>
(and) <u>they should get plenty of exercise.</u>

_____[words]_____ 5. I need some <u>exercise</u> (and) <u>sunshine</u>.

**D.** Circle the correct interjection.

1. ( Good! (Oh, no!) ) We're out of popcorn.

2. Tomorrow is a holiday! ( (Hooray!) Ouch! )

3. ( (Look!) Yum! ) That car crashed into a telephone pole!

4. There's a free concert in the park after school today. ( (Great!) Oops! )

5. ( Look! (Listen!) ) They're playing my favorite song on the radio!

## Try It Yourself
Write four sentences about your eating habits and preferences.
Be sure to use prepositions, conjunctions, and interjections correctly.

_____

_____

_____

_____

## Check Your Own Work
Choose a selection from your writing portfolio, your journal, a work in progress,
an assignment from another subject, or a letter. Revise it, applying the skills
you have reviewed. The checklist will help you.

✔ Have you used prepositional phrases to give details about
your ideas?

✔ Did you use commas when using a coordinating conjunction to
join independent clauses?

✔ Have you chosen the appropriate interjections to express your
feelings or emotions?

**Prepositions, Conjunctions, Interjections**

Name _____

# 108. Reviewing Parts of Speech—Part 1

On the line write whether the underlined word in each sentence is a **noun**, **pronoun**, **verb**, **adjective**, **adverb**, **preposition**, **conjunction**, or **interjection**.

[verb] _____ 1. Eleanor Roosevelt was one of the most admired and influential first ladies of the United States.

[adjective] _____ 2. She was born into a wealthy New York family that placed great value on education and public service.

[adverb] _____ 3. She studied in England and later worked hard as a teacher in a settlement house on New York's Lower East Side.

[conjunction] _____ 4. In 1905 she married Franklin Roosevelt and helped him in his career as a New York politician.

[noun] _____ 5. Her husband became governor of New York.

[adverb] _____ 6. After Franklin Roosevelt became president of the United States, she took a very active role.

[preposition] _____ 7. The country was suffering from the effects of the Great Depression of 1929, and many people were out of work.

[adjective] _____ 8. Living conditions for many Americans were difficult.

[conjunction] _____ 9. Mrs. Roosevelt visited the poor and reported on conditions to her husband.

[pronoun] _____ 10. She visited miners, farmers, and factory workers in every part of the country.

[adjective] _____ 11. She also worked hard to win equal rights for women and minorities.

[adverb] _____ 12. For example, Marian Anderson, an African-American opera singer, was not allowed to sing in a Washington, D.C., concert hall.

[pronoun] _____ 13. Mrs. Roosevelt organized a concert for her at the Lincoln Memorial.

[noun] _____ 14. After President Roosevelt died in office in 1945, President Truman named her U.S. representative to the United Nations.

[interjection] _____ 15. She continued to work for human rights until her death in 1962. Hooray for Eleanor Roosevelt!

 Eleanor Roosevelt believed in service to the community. What organizations help people in your community? Give an example of something you can do to help them.

# 109. Reviewing Parts of Speech—Part 2

**A.** Circle the correct choice in parentheses for the underlined words in the sentences.

1. <u>Betty</u>, who killed President Lincoln?  ( subject (direct address) )

2. John Wilkes Booth <u>shot</u> him in 1865.  ( (past tense) past perfect tense )

3. Booth <u>was</u> an actor from the South.  ( transitive (linking) )

4. He was angry that the South had lost the war, <u>and</u> he hated Lincoln.  ( (conjunction) preposition )

5. He found out that Lincoln <u>might</u> attend the theater one night.  ( (auxiliary) transitive )

6. Lincoln wanted to see a famous <u>actress</u> in a play.  ( (common) proper )

7. The play was <u>very</u> funny.  ( (degree) manner )

8. <u>Suddenly</u> a shot rang out.  ( (manner) negation )

9. Booth escaped, but <u>he</u> hurt his leg.  ( (third person) first person )

10. The president was <u>dead</u>.  ( (subject complement) direct object )

**B.** On the line supply the information about the underlined word(s) in each sentence.

1. <u>Who</u> is this book about?  kind of pronoun  _____ [interrogative]

2. <u>This</u> book is about Lincoln.  kind of adjective  _____ [demonstrative]

3. I will <u>read</u> it tonight.  tense of verb  _____ [future]

4. <u>He</u> was the sixteenth president of the United States.  person of pronoun  _____ [third]

5. It was <u>not</u> an easy time to be president.  kind of adverb  _____ [negation]

6. A <u>bloody</u> Civil War broke out over slavery.  part of speech  _____ [adjective]

7. The North <u>and</u> the South went to war in 1861.  part of speech  _____ [conjunction]

8. The Northern army finally <u>won</u>.  tense of verb  _____ [past]

9. <u>Alas!</u> Lincoln did not live to rebuild the country.  part of speech  _____ [interjection]

10. He died <u>of</u> an assassin's bullet.  part of speech  _____ [preposition]

Phrases, Clauses, Sentences

116

# 110. Reviewing Parts of Speech—Part 3

> Adjectives and adverbs are modifiers. Adjectives describe nouns or pronouns.
> Adverbs modify verbs, adjectives, or other adverbs.

**A.** The underlined words are adjectives. Circle the word each one describes.
On the line write the part of speech of that word.

_____[noun]_____ 1. Hans Christian Andersen is a famous (writer) of fairy tales.

_____[noun]_____ 2. He lived in the 19th (century).

_____[pronoun]_____ 3. (He) was Danish.

_____[noun]_____ 4. Hans came from a poor (family).

_____[noun]_____ 5. His (fairy tales) were successful and earned him a good living.

**B.** Each underlined word is an adverb. Circle the word each modifies.
On the line write the part of speech of that word.

_____[verb]_____ 1. Andersen (wrote) extensively.

_____[adjective]_____ 2. He left a very (large) number of tales.

_____[verb]_____ 3. Many of his tales (end) unhappily.

_____[adverb]_____ 4. Both children and adults respond quite (emotionally) to his tales.

_____[verb]_____ 5. People frequently (have made) his tales into films, plays, or ballets.

**C.** Above each underlined word, write **Adj** if it is an adjective or **Adv** if it is an adverb. Circle the word it modifies. Above the modified word, write its part of speech.

1. One of Andersen's [Adj] popular [Noun] (tales) is "The Ugly Duckling."

2. A poor [Noun] (duck) is [Adj] unhappy because he isn't like his brother and sisters.

3. He [Adv] slowly [Verb] (grows) up, and he turns into a lovely swan, not a duck at all.

4. Andersen's tales [Adv] often [Verb] (teach) the lesson of accepting what you are.

5. He wrote a [Adv] quite [Adj] (funny) tale about a princess called "The Princess and the Pea."

6. A prince is searching for the [Adj] perfect [Noun] (princess).

7. A [Adj] young [Noun] (princess) visits the prince's family.

8. Servants [Verb] (pile) 20 mattresses [Adv] high—with a pea at the very bottom—for her bed.

9. The next morning the princess has not slept [Adv] very [Adv] (well)—because of the pea.

10. [Pronoun] (She) is very [Adj] sensitive, and so she is the perfect princess for the prince.

Name_____

# 111. Identifying Adjectival Phrases

An **adjectival phrase** is a prepositional phrase used as an adjective.
**I read an article about the environment.**

**A.** Underline the adjectival phrase in each sentence.
Circle the noun each one modifies.

1. Killer (bees) from Africa are invading the Americas.

2. (People) in Brazil brought them originally.

3. They wanted an (increase) in honey production.

4. The (spread) of the killer bees is occurring gradually.

5. (Areas) of Texas, Arizona, and California now have these bees.

6. The killers are fierce (defenders) of their nests.

7. They will immediately attack any nearby (source) of movement.

8. Numerous bees might join together and make an (attack) on a person.

9. One (defense) against these bees is running.

10. But (pursuit) by these bees can continue up to one mile!

**B.** Rewrite each group of words as an adjectival phrase.

| | | |
|---|---|---|
| United States flag | 1. | [flag of the United States] |
| children's drawings | 2. | [drawings by the children] |
| forest animals | 3. | [animals in the forest] |
| wolf's den | 4. | [den of the wolf] |
| animal's tracks | 5. | [tracks of the animal] |
| house plants | 6. | [plants in the house] |
| jungle adventures | 7. | [adventures in the jungle] |
| leopard's spots | 8. | [spots of the leopard] |
| soccer rules | 9. | [rules of soccer] |
| piano keys | 10. | [keys of the piano] |

Phrases, Clauses, Sentences

# 112. Writing Adjectival Phrases

**A.** Complete each sentence with an adjectival phrase using the noun at the left.     **[Answers will vary.]**

distance     1. That peak _____[in the distance]_____ is Pike's Peak.

courage     2. The world will always need leaders _____[with courage]_____.

Brazil     3. Coffee _____[from Brazil]_____ is shipped to the United States.

ice     4. The sidewalk glistened in its coat _____[of ice]_____.

California     5. Many movies are made in the film studios _____[of/in California]_____.

intelligence     6. Eleanor Roosevelt was a woman _____[of/with intelligence]_____.

France     7. The United States asked the government _____[of France]_____ for help.

strength     8. Only a person _____[with strength]_____ could move this piano alone.

fear     9. This assignment requires a soldier _____[without fear]_____.

Poland     10. The flight _____[to/for/from Poland]_____ took off at 10:00 this morning.

**B.** Complete each sentence with an adjectival phrase.

1. The fire _____[Answers will vary.]_____ caused a great deal of damage.

2. The cheers _____ filled the theater.

3. Hugh is the best player _____.

4. The president _____ gave a report to Congress.

5. The flowers _____ are beautifully arranged.

6. The road _____ is very narrow.

7. The door _____ is open.

8. The principal _____ made an announcement.

9. The Bill of Rights guarantees freedom _____.

10. The food _____ was delicious.

Phrases, Clauses, Sentences

119

# 113. Identifying Adverbial Phrases

> An **adverbial phrase** is a phrase used as an adverb.
> The United States and Canada are located <u>in North America</u>.

**A.** Underline the adverbial phrases.

1. Buffalo once roamed <u>over the Great Plains</u>.

2. Corn and wheat grow <u>in the Midwest</u>.

3. The Ohio and Missouri Rivers flow <u>into the Mississippi River</u>.

4. Many large cities lie <u>along these rivers</u>.

5. The eastern rim of the plains is formed <u>by the Appalachian Mountains</u>.

6. <u>Across the plains</u> the Rockies and the Sierra Nevadas form the western boundary.

7. Settlers crossed the Great Plains <u>in covered wagons</u>.

8. They built towns <u>in valleys and along rivers</u>.

9. They often lived <u>in simple log cabins</u>.

10. Pioneers sometimes encountered danger <u>in their new homes</u>.

11. Wolves, bears, and coyotes often lived <u>in nearby forests</u>.

12. Settlers farmed <u>during the summer</u>.

13. <u>In the winter</u> they cleared land.

14. Early settlers built towns <u>throughout the plains</u>.

15. Look <u>on the map</u> and find these locations.

**B.** Write sentences replacing the underlined adverb with an adverbial phrase. **[Sentences will vary.]**

lived <u>peacefully</u>    1. ____ [lived in peace] _____

moved <u>westward</u>    2. ____ [moved to/toward the west] _____

grew <u>swiftly</u>    3. ____ [grew with swiftness] _____

drove <u>carefully</u>    4. ____ [drove with care] _____

listened <u>silently</u>    5. ____ [listened in silence] _____

**Phrases, Clauses, Sentences**

Name_____

# 114. Writing Adverbial Phrases

**A.** Complete each sentence with an adverbial phrase. **[Answers will vary.]**

1. The audience laughed _____.

2. _____ our family visits my grandmother.

3. The airplane landed _____.

4. Can you be ready _____?

5. Yesterday afternoon they played ball _____.

6. Kelly lost her backpack _____.

7. I put the candy _____.

8. Flowers grow _____.

9. I sometimes watch TV _____.

10. He parked the car _____.

11. We ate lunch _____.

12. The teacher collected the papers _____.

13. A fire truck drove up _____.

14. Please put the dishes away _____.

15. Hang your coat _____.

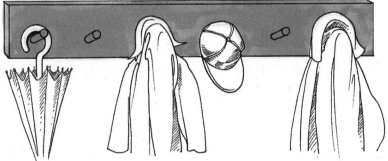

**B.** Use each adverbial phrase in a sentence.

at all times       1. _____**[Sentences will vary.]**_____

in the park       2. _____

at five o'clock       3. _____

in the living room    4. _____

at school       5. _____

**121**

# 115. Distinguishing Between Adjectival and Adverbial Phrases

An adjectival phrase modifies a noun or a pronoun.
An adverbial phrase modifies a verb, an adjective, or an adverb.

ADJECTIVAL PHRASE
**Earth is the third *planet* of the solar system. (modifies *planet*)**

ADVERBIAL PHRASE
**The moon *circles* Earth in a regular orbit. (modifies *circles*)**

**A.** Underline the phrases in each sentence. Above each write **Adj** if the phrase is adjectival or **Adv** if it is adverbial.

1. You are seeing Earth from space. [Adv]

2. Earth is the fifth largest planet of our solar system. [Adj]

3. Land and water can be seen on Earth's surface. [Adv]

4. The greatest amount of land lies in the Northern Hemisphere. [Adj] [Adv]

5. The view from space shows the oceans on Earth. [Adj] [Adj]

6. Water covers most of Earth's surface. [Adj]

7. Land divides the water into four major oceans. [Adv]

8. The system of oceans has many connections. [Adj]

9. Earth's land is divided into seven continents. [Adv]

10. The continent with the largest area is Asia. [Adj]

**B.** Complete each sentence with an adjectival or an adverbial phrase. On the line at the left write **Adj** if the phrase is adjectival or **Adv** if it is adverbial.

[Adv] 1. Yesterday our class went ___[Answers will vary.]___ .

[Adv] 2. I study best _____ .

[Adv] 3. A heavy fog hung _____ .

[Adj] 4. The cheers _____ filled the stadium.

[Adj] 5. Lauren is the best soccer player _____ .

[Adv] 6. Colonists settled _____ .

[Adv] 7. We drove _____ .

[Adv] 8. The teacher wrote quickly _____ .

[Adj] 9. The present _____ is for you!

[Adj] 10. The sneakers _____ are very nice.

# 116. Identifying Natural and Inverted Order

A sentence is in **natural order** when the verb follows the subject.

SUBJECT     VERB
**The Spanish *conquerors* came onto the island.**

A sentence is in **inverted order** when the verb or an auxiliary comes before the subject.

VERB                    SUBJECT
**Onto the island came the Spanish *conquerors*.**

VERB          SUBJECT        VERB
**When did the Spanish *conquerors* come onto the island?**

**A.** Underline the subject once and the verb twice. On the line write **N** if the sentence is in natural order or **I** if it is in inverted order.

__[N]__ 1. Europeans first <u>came</u> to the Americas in 1492.

__[I]__ 2. To the Americas <u>came</u> explorers, missionaries, and settlers.

__[N]__ 3. Spain <u>conquered</u> much of Mexico, Central America, and South America.

__[I]__ 4. In the rest of North America <u>lived</u> settlers from England and France.

__[N]__ 5. The newly arrived Europeans <u>uprooted</u> and destroyed the Native American civilizations.

__[I]__ 6. Westward <u>pushed</u> the North American pioneers.

__[I]__ 7. To reservations <u>went</u> Native Americans.

__[N]__ 8. The Cherokee <u>traveled</u> from Georgia to the West on a journey later called "The Trail of Tears."

__[I]__ 9. Did the Sioux move to a reservation?

__[N]__ 10. Early settlers <u>focused</u> on their expansionist needs and not on the needs of the native people.

**B.** Five of the sentences in Part A are in inverted order. Rewrite them in natural order on the lines.

1. _____ [Explorers, missionaries, and settlers came to the Americas.] _____

2. _____ [Settlers from England and France lived in the rest of North America.] _____

3. _____ [The North American pioneers pushed westward.] _____

4. _____ [Native Americans went to reservations.] _____

5. _____ [The Sioux did move to a reservation.] _____

Name_____

# 117. Using Natural and Inverted Order

**A.** Rewrite each sentence using inverted order.
Use inverted order in questions where indicated.

1. Abner Doubleday invented the game of baseball. *(question)*

   [Did Abner Doubleday invent the game of baseball?]

2. The annual All-Star Game began in 1933.

   [In 1933 began the annual All-Star Game.]

3. Wrigley Field, the home of the Chicago Cubs, is here.

   [Here is Wrigley Field, the home of the Chicago Cubs.]

4. The Baseball Hall of Fame stands in Cooperstown, New York.

   [In Cooperstown, New York, stands the Baseball Hall of Fame.]

5. Hank Aaron's bat is among the baseball relics in the hall. *(question)*

   [Is Hank Aaron's bat among the baseball relics

   in the hall?]

**B.** Rewrite each sentence using natural order.

1. Does he know when the sport of baseball began?

   [He does know when the sport of baseball began.]

2. Named to the Baseball Hall of Fame in 1973 was Roberto Clemente.

   [Roberto Clemente was named to the Baseball Hall of Fame in 1973.]

3. Into the air leapt the star outfielder.

   [The star outfielder leapt into the air.]

4. In the bottom of the ninth inning came the last desperate attempt to win.

   [The last desperate attempt to win came in the bottom of the ninth inning.]

5. Into home plate slid the runner with the winning run.

   [The runner with the winning run slid into home plate.]

Phrases, Clauses, Sentences

124

# 118. Identifying Simple Sentences

A **simple sentence** contains a subject and a predicate.
Either or both may be compound.

| SUBJECT | PREDICATE |
|---|---|
| Lyndon Johnson | had a long record of public service. |
| Johnson <u>and</u> his wife, Lady Bird, | were from Texas. |
| Johnson | worked hard for civil right laws <u>and</u> tried to help poor Americans. |

**A.** Underline the simple subject(s) once.
Underline the simple predicate(s) twice.
Identify compound subject(s) and predicate(s)
by writing **C** in the appropriate column(s).

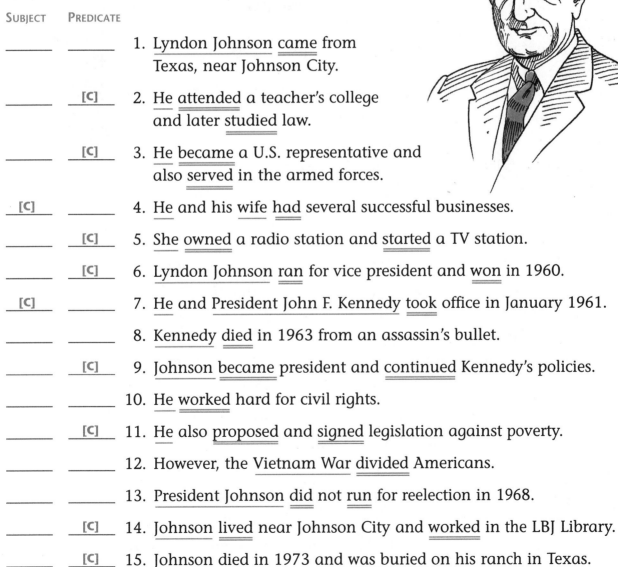

SUBJECT   PREDICATE

_____   _____   1. Lyndon <u>Johnson</u> <u><u>came</u></u> from Texas, near Johnson City.

_____   [C]   2. <u>He</u> <u><u>attended</u></u> a teacher's college and later <u><u>studied</u></u> law.

_____   [C]   3. <u>He</u> <u><u>became</u></u> a U.S. representative and also <u><u>served</u></u> in the armed forces.

[C]   _____   4. <u>He</u> and his <u>wife</u> <u><u>had</u></u> several successful businesses.

_____   [C]   5. <u>She</u> <u><u>owned</u></u> a radio station and <u><u>started</u></u> a TV station.

_____   [C]   6. Lyndon <u>Johnson</u> <u><u>ran</u></u> for vice president and <u><u>won</u></u> in 1960.

[C]   _____   7. <u>He</u> and President John F. <u>Kennedy</u> <u><u>took</u></u> office in January 1961.

_____   _____   8. <u>Kennedy</u> <u><u>died</u></u> in 1963 from an assassin's bullet.

_____   [C]   9. <u>Johnson</u> <u><u>became</u></u> president and <u><u>continued</u></u> Kennedy's policies.

_____   _____   10. <u>He</u> <u><u>worked</u></u> hard for civil rights.

_____   [C]   11. <u>He</u> also <u><u>proposed</u></u> and <u><u>signed</u></u> legislation against poverty.

_____   _____   12. However, the Vietnam <u>War</u> <u><u>divided</u></u> Americans.

_____   _____   13. President <u>Johnson</u> <u><u>did</u></u> not <u><u>run</u></u> for reelection in 1968.

_____   [C]   14. <u>Johnson</u> <u><u>lived</u></u> near Johnson City and <u><u>worked</u></u> in the LBJ Library.

_____   [C]   15. <u>Johnson</u> <u><u>died</u></u> in 1973 and was <u><u>buried</u></u> on his ranch in Texas.

# 119.  Identifying Compound Sentences

A **compound sentence** contains two or more independent clauses.
An independent clause has a subject and a verb and can stand on
its own as a sentence. Independent clauses are usually connected by
the coordinating conjunctions *and, but, or, nor, yet, for,* and *so.*

INDEPENDENT CLAUSE                                    INDEPENDENT CLAUSE
**Albany is the capital of New York, but New York City is its largest city.**

A semicolon may be used between independent clauses
instead of a coordinating conjunction.

**Albany is the capital of New York; New York City is its largest city.**

**A.**  In each compound sentence underline the simple subjects once
and the verbs twice. Circle the coordinating conjunction or the semicolon.

1. New York City has the most inhabitants of any city in the United States,
   (but) Los Angeles covers more land.

2. New York City is the largest city in the United States,
   (and) Los Angeles is the second largest.

3. New York City sits on a number of islands and bays,
   (and) the most famous island is Manhattan.

4. San Francisco is located in northern California, (and)
   Los Angeles is located in southern California.

5. Los Angeles has many TV (and) film studios, and San Francisco
   has many banks and financial service companies.

6. San Francisco is fairly hilly(;) Los Angeles is more level.

7. Los Angeles and New York City are located on coasts(;) Chicago is inland.

8. New York City has many tall buildings, (but) Chicago has the tallest building
   in the country.

9. In Los Angeles many people drive cars, (and) in New York many people use subways.

10. Each city is different(;) the cities all are special in their own way.

**B.**  Write **S** if the sentence is simple or **C** if the sentence is compound.
Then add the correct punctuation to each compound sentence.

__[S]__  1. New York is famous for its large number of theaters.

__[C]__  2. New York has several orchestras, and it has several ballet companies too.

__[C]__  3. The Statue of Liberty is in New York Harbor; millions of people visit it yearly.

__[S]__  4. New York City is a business center and is the home of many banks.

__[C]__  5. The New York skyline is famous, and Central Park is a great escape from the
   hustle and bustle of the city.

# 120. Writing Compound Sentences

Combine each pair of simple sentences to form a compound sentence.
Use a comma before the coordinating conjunctions *and*, *but*, *or*, *nor*, *yet*, *for*, or *so*.

1. The United States celebrates its Independence Day on July 4th. Peru celebrates its Independence Day on July 28th.

   [The United States celebrates its Independence Day on July 4th, and/but

   Peru celebrates its Independence Day on July 28th.]

2. Americans might attend fireworks displays on July 4th. They might stay at home and watch them on TV.

   [Americans might attend fireworks displays on July 4th, or they might stay

   at home and watch them on TV.]

3. Many countries celebrate New Year's Day on January 1. In Muslim countries New Year's is the first day of the month of Muharram.

   [Many countries celebrate New Year's Day on January 1, but in Muslim countries,

   New Year's is the first day of the month of Muharram.]

4. On New Year's Day many Americans watch football games on TV. On that day many Chinese visit friends and exchange gifts.

   [On New Year's Day many Americans watch football games on TV, but on that day

   many Chinese visit friends and exchange gifts.]

5. In the United States Mother's Day is in May. Father's Day is in June.

   [In the United States Mother's Day is in May, and Father's Day is in June.]

6. Brazil's Carnival is right before Lent. New Orleans' Mardi Gras is at that same time.

   [Brazil's Carnival is right before Lent, and New Orleans' Mardi Gras is at that same time.]

7. In most western countries Sunday is a holiday. In Islamic countries Friday is a holiday.

   [In most western countries Sunday is a holiday, and/but in Islamic countries Friday

   is a holiday.]

8. The Queen of England's birthday is a holiday in England. This day is not a holiday in the United States.

   [The Queen of England's birthday is a holiday in England, but this day is not a holiday

   in the United States.]

9. Queen Elizabeth's real birthday is April 21st. People celebrate her birthday on the third Saturday in June, when the weather in England is warmer.

   [Queen Elizabeth's real birthday is April 21st, but people celebrate her birthday

   on the third Saturday in June, when the weather in England is warmer.]

10. The Christian holiday of Easter is usually in April. Sometimes it is in March.

    [The Christian holiday of Easter is usually in April, and/but sometimes it is in March.]

# 121. Reviewing Simple and Compound Sentences

On the line write **S** if a sentence is simple or **C** if it is compound.

_[C]_ 1. Fairy tales are fictitious, but they are excellent stories.

_[S]_ 2. In Germany the Grimm Brothers collected many fairy tales.

_[C]_ 3. Jacob Grimm was born in 1785, and Wilhelm Grimm was born in 1786.

_[S]_ 4. Jacob and Wilhelm studied law in college at first.

_[C]_ 5. They developed a love of German folk traditions from their teachers, and they began to study folktales and fairy stories.

_[C]_ 6. Many of these stories were very old; some dated from the Middle Ages or earlier.

_[C]_ 7. The brothers became lawyers, but they remained interested in these stories.

_[S]_ 8. By 1814 they gave up their legal careers and pursued their studies of folktales.

_[C]_ 9. They did not make very much money, and they had to spend their earnings very carefully.

_[S]_ 10. They collected large numbers of stories and published them in a book.

_[S]_ 11. Some of the stories in their collection are versions of Cinderella and Rapunzel.

_[C]_ 12. This book was popular, and thousands of people bought copies.

_[S]_ 13. In 1840 the king invited the brothers to Berlin.

_[C]_ 14. In Berlin the king paid them a generous salary, and they could focus on their work.

_[S]_ 15. Wilhelm and Jacob also began to study linguistics and published an important book about the German language.

_[C]_ 16. They also started work on a German dictionary, but the task was too large for them.

_[C]_ 17. Wilhelm finished only to the letter D by the time of his death, and Jacob reached only F.

_[S]_ 18. Their collections of stories and their other books made the brothers famous.

_[S]_ 19. They received prizes and honors.

_[S]_ 20. They are most beloved for their collections of fairy stories and folktales.

Name_____

# 122. Reviewing Phrases, Clauses, and Sentences

**A.** Identify the use of each underlined phrase.
Write **Adj** if it is adjectival or **Adv** if it is adverbial.

___[Adv]___  1. The common cold can be caused <u>by many different viruses</u>.

___[Adv]___  2. Usually a cold virus is caught <u>from another person</u>.

___[Adj]___  3. Infections <u>in the throat</u> can lead to coughs.

___[Adj]___  4. Cough medicine can reduce the amount <u>of discomfort</u>
         a person experiences.

___[Adj]___  5. So far no one has invented a cure <u>for the common cold</u>.

**B.** Underline the simple subject(s) in each sentence once. Underline
the simple predicate(s) twice. A subject or a predicate may be compound.

 1. <u>Microbes</u> <u>grow</u> or <u>multiply</u> on most foods.

 2. <u>Is</u> the <u>infection</u> or <u>disease</u> bacterial or viral?

 3. The <u>conditions</u> and <u>requirements</u> for their growth <u>vary</u>.

 4. <u>Warmth</u>, <u>moisture</u>, and a <u>source</u> of food <u>are</u> necessary to most organisms.

 5. In the kitchen, <u>microbes</u> <u>can cause</u> food poisoning.

 6. A few <u>steps</u> <u>can reduce</u> or <u>eliminate</u> the chances of food poisoning.

 7. <u>Meat</u> and <u>poultry</u> <u>should be stored</u> properly and <u>cooked</u> completely.

 8. <u>People</u> <u>should refrigerate</u> leftover food promptly.

 9. <u>Everyone</u> <u>should wash</u> his or her hands before cooking or eating.

10. <u>People</u> <u>should</u> also <u>wash</u> dishes in hot, soapy water.

**C.** On the line write **S** if a sentence is simple
or **C** if it is compound.

___[C]___  1. Nutrients give you energy, and they are
        essential for growth and good health.

___[S]___  2. Select foods from a variety of food groups.

___[C]___  3. Fats give your body energy, but protein builds
        and repairs.

___[S]___  4. Oranges and grapefruit are excellent sources of vitamin C.

___[S]___  5. Milk and milk products such as yogurt and cheese supply
        calcium, protein, and several vitamins.

Phrases, Clauses, Sentences

129

Name_____

**D.** On the line write **N** if the sentence is in natural order or **I** if it is in inverted order. Then rewrite the sentence to change its order.

___[I]___ 1. Did he hear about the swim meet at the park yesterday?

[He did hear about the swim meet at the park yesterday.]

___[N]___ 2. Children from all over the city competed in the meet.

[In the meet competed children from all over the city.]

___[I]___ 3. Awarded the first prize was Elena Hernandez.

[Elena Hernandez was awarded the first prize.]

___[I]___ 4. Onto the winner's podium stepped a smiling Elena.

[A smiling Elena stepped onto the winner's podium.]

___[I]___ 5. Will Elena compete in the city-wide meet next month?

[Elena will compete in the

city-wide meet next month.]

## Try It Yourself
Write four sentences about your favorite book or folktale.
Be sure to use prepositions, conjunctions, and interjections correctly.

_____

_____

_____

_____

## Check Your Own Work
Choose a selection from your writing portfolio, your journal,
a work in progress, an assignment from another subject, or a letter.
Revise it, applying the skills you have reviewed. The checklist will help you.

✔ Have you chosen adjectival and adverbial phrases that give detail
to your descriptions?

✔ Have you corrected any incomplete sentences?

✔ Have you used conjunctions and commas to join compound sentences?

✔ Does your piece have variety in sentence order?

Name

# 123. Using Periods and Question Marks

> A **period** is used at the end of a declarative sentence and after an abbreviation or an initial.
>
> **Dr. Albert Einstein is one of the most important scientists of all time.**
>
> Use a **question mark** at the end of every question.
>
> **Where was Einstein born?**

**Add a period or a question mark where needed.**

1. Who discovered the theory of relativity ?

2. Albert Einstein announced it in 1905 .

3. Did people realize that Einstein's theory was revolutionary ?

4. No, it took a number of years for people to realize the importance of this breakthrough .

5. Einstein's life was drastically affected by war .

6. World War I separated him from his wife and children, who were in Switzerland when war broke out .

7. What happened to Einstein when the Nazis came to power ?

8. Einstein renounced his German citizenship and left the country .

9. Did he do anything to stop the Nazis ?

10. He organized protests against the Nazi government and urged countries to be ready in case war broke out .

11. When did he win the Nobel Prize ?

12. He won it in 1921 .

13. After he left Germany, he moved to the United States and became a U.S.citizen .

14. Einstein continued his work until his death in 1955 .

15. In my father's library I found a book titled *Einstein: The Man and His Achievement* by G.J.Whitrow .

Einstein made important discoveries in science. If you were a scientist, what would you like to discover? Give an example of how your discoveries could help the world.

# 124. Using Exclamation Points

> Use an **exclamation point** at the end of an exclamatory sentence and after an interjection.
>
> **What a genius Einstein was!**
> **Oh, no! I left my report on Einstein at home.**

**A.** Insert a period or an exclamation point where needed.

1. Shh! The baby is sleeping .
2. What a great movie !
3. Today is a snow day! Hooray !
4. I put the brownies on the table .
5. The bus is coming. Hurry !
6. I got up on time today .
7. Juanita makes delicious cookies .
8. Tomorrow is Tuesday .
9. We visited my aunt and uncle on Sunday .
10. It's very cold out. Don't open that door !

**B.** Insert a period, question mark, or exclamation point where needed.

1. What is a peninsula ?
2. Spain, Italy, and Greece are located on peninsulas .
3. What is the difference between a peninsula and an island ?
4. Which U.S. state is located on a group of islands ?
5. Wow! It's really far from the other states .
6. Alaska has a group of islands too .
7. Several places on the coast of South Carolina are islands only when the tide is high .
8. When the tide is low, they are connected to the mainland by sandbars .
9. Really! Can you drive to those islands ?
10. Yes, the sandbars are quite compact, and a small car can drive on them .

# 125. Using Commas in Series, Dates, and Addresses

**Commas** are used to separate words or groups of words in a series of three or more and to set off parts of dates, addresses, and geographic names.

**Illinois produces corn, soybeans, and wheat.**

**Springfield, Illinois, was Lincoln's home for many years.**

**Illinois joined the Union on December 3, 1818, as the twenty-first state.**

**The John Hancock Building, the tallest apartment building in the world, is located at 875 North Michigan Avenue, Chicago, Illinois 60611.**

**A.** Insert commas where needed.

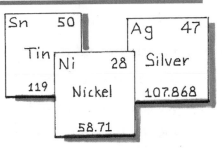

1. Silver, mercury, tin, and nickel are metals.
2. These metals are found in the United States, South Africa, and Canada.
3. Coal, oil, and natural gas are fossil fuels.
4. The United States imports petroleum from Venezuela, Saudi Arabia, and Kuwait.
5. Acid rain from burning fossil fuels harms plants, animals, and people.
6. Fossil fuels are obtained by drilling, strip-mining, and tunneling.
7. The United States needs to explore alternative kinds of energy, such as solar power, wind power, and nuclear power.
8. Geysers, volcanoes, and tides are other natural sources of energy.
9. A fuel called methanol can be obtained from wood, coal, and natural gas.
10. In the meantime people mine coal, dig oil wells, and transport natural gas.

**B.** Rewrite the sentences and insert commas where needed.

1. The United States adopted the Constitution on September 17 1787.

   [The United States adopted the Constitution on September 17, 1787.]

2. Philadelphia Pennsylvania was where the Constitution was written.

   [Philadelphia, Pennsylvania, was where the Constitution was written.]

3. Boonesboro Kentucky reportedly was founded by Daniel Boone on April 1 1775.

   [Boonesboro, Kentucky, reportedly was founded by Daniel Boone on April 1, 1775.]

4. The White House is at 1600 Pennsylvania Avenue Washington D.C.

   [The White House is at 1600 Pennsylvania Avenue, Washington, D.C.]

5. The *Mayflower* landed at what is now Plymouth Massachusetts on December 21 1620.

   [The *Mayflower* landed at what is now Plymouth, Massachusetts, on December 21, 1620.]

Punctuation & Capitalization

133

Name_____

# 126. Using Commas with Yes, No, and Direct Address

> Commas are used to set off *yes* and *no* when they introduce sentences, and they are used to set off words in direct address.
>
> **Yes, Marie Curie discovered both polonium and radium.**
> **Jeff, Marie Curie was a famous scientist.**

**A.** Insert commas where needed.

1. No Marie Curie was not born in France.

2. Yes she moved to Paris in 1891.

3. No she was not very rich.

4. Yes she had to work hard to get an education.

5. Yes she began to study physics at the university.

6. Yes she met her future husband, Pierre Curie, at the university in 1894.

7. No she didn't win her first Nobel Prize alone.

8. Yes she won it in 1903 with her husband and another scientist.

9. Yes she received her doctoral degree that year too.

10. No she didn't stop her work when her husband died in 1906.

**B.** Insert commas where needed.

1. Marie Curie class was an important woman scientist.

2. She was the first woman to teach at the Sorbonne Christine.

3. Marie Curie studied medical uses of radiation everyone at one time.

4. In 1921 she traveled to the United States Mary Jane.

5. The president presented Curie class with a gram of radium.

6. That radium students had been purchased with money collected by American women all over the country.

7. The women collected that money because they wanted to help her with her work Josh.

8. Unfortunately Gerardo Marie Curie became sick because of her contact with radioactive elements.

9. At that time Soo-Ha nobody realized that excessive exposure to radiation could be dangerous.

10. Marie Curie class is buried in Paris near other great French heroes.

# 127. Using Commas in Letters and with Appositives

Commas are used after the salutation in a social or friendly letter and after the complimentary close in all letters.

**Dear Aunt Helen,** *(after salutation)*

**Thanks for the video games you gave me for my birthday. I play them every day after I finish my homework.**

**Love,** *(after complimentary close)*
**Bradley**

Commas are used to set off an appositive.

**William the Conqueror, the first Norman king of England, gained control of England in 1066.**

**A.** Insert commas where needed.

**Dear Aunt Marge and Uncle Ralph ,**

**Thanks for taking Billy and me camping last week. It was really fun to visit Yellowstone Park and see the bears and geysers. I hope you can spend Christmas with us again this year.**

**Love ,**
**Paula**

**B.** Insert commas where needed.

1. Queen Elizabeth, the present queen of England, ascended the throne on February 6, 1952.

2. The queen's father, George VI, had been king from 1936 to 1952.

3. George VI became king when his brother, Edward VIII, abdicated in order to marry Wallis Simpson, an American woman.

4. George VI and Elizabeth, his wife, courageously stayed in London during the bombings of World War II.

5. Queen Elizabeth is married to Phillip Mountbatten, the Duke of Edinburgh.

6. Prince Charles, her son, is next in line to the throne.

7. Prince Charles, the Prince of Wales, was married to Diana Spencer.

8. Diana, the Princess of Wales, died in a tragic automobile accident in Paris in 1997.

9. The eldest son of Charles and Diana, Prince William, is second in line for the throne.

10. Some people think that the English monarchy may end upon the death of the present sovereign, Queen Elizabeth.

# 128. Using Commas with Quotations

Commas are used to set off short direct quotations from the rest of the sentence. If the quotation is at the beginning of the sentence, place a comma after the last word of the quotation, unless a question mark or an exclamation point is needed.

**"Mexico is the United States' neighbor to the south," said Professor Louis.**

If the quotation is at the end of the sentence, place a comma after the last word before the quotation.

**Professor Louis said, "Mexico is the United States' neighbor to the south."**

If the quotation is divided, use a comma after the first part and before the last part.

**"Mexico," Professor Louis said, "is the United States' neighbor to the south."**

**Insert commas where needed.**

1. "Mexico," said Professor Louis, "has a long and rich history."

2. "The original inhabitants of Mexico were Native Americans of various groups such as Aztecs and Toltecs," he said.

3. "These indigenous groups built important civilizations," he continued.

4. A student asked, "What happened to these civilizations?"

5. "They changed dramatically," he answered, "when the Spanish arrived starting in 1492."

6. He stated, "By 1535 Mexico was completely under Spanish control."

7. "During the colonial period many indigenous achievements were forgotten or lost," he said.

8. "What a terrible thing!" the class exclaimed.

9. The professor told the students, "Mexico declared its independence from Spain in 1810."

10. "However," he continued, "Spain did not recognize Mexico's independence until 1821."

11. "Mexico had several forms of government," he explained, "in the following years, including a republican government and an empire."

12. One student asked, "What is Mexico like today?"

13. "Nowadays," said the professor, "Mexico is a developing country with rich cultural traditions."

14. "Mexico is rich in mineral wealth, and it is an important manufacturing center," he said.

15. "Tourism is an important business as well," concluded the professor.

# 129. Using Commas in Compound Sentences

> Commas are used to separate the clauses of a compound sentence connected by the coordinating conjunctions *and*, *but*, *or*, *nor*, and *yet*.
>
> **The Atlantic Ocean is east of the United States, and the Pacific Ocean is west.**

**A.** Insert commas where needed. If no comma is needed, write **NC** on the line.

_____ 1. The longest river in the United States is the Mississippi but the Nile River is longer.

_____ 2. The Great Lakes are the world's largest freshwater system and the Mississippi River is the world's largest navigable river system.

_____ 3. The rivers of Japan are short but have many waterfalls.

_____ 4. The most important rivers in northern Europe are the Danube and the Rhine.

_____ 5. The Amazon River is the longest river in South America and the Paraná is the second-longest.

_____ 6. The Congo River is the longest river in sub-Saharan Africa but the Nile River in Egypt is longer.

_____ 7. The Yangtze River is the longest river in China and in all of Asia.

_____ 8. People use rivers to generate electricity and rivers also serve as a means of transportation.

_____ 9. Rivers are a source of water for drinking and for the irrigation of crops.

_____ 10. This summer I will sail the Mississippi River or I will take a cruise on the Amazon.

**B.** Complete each sentence with a coordinating conjunction and a comma if required.

1. Root beer was a type of herbal tea _____ later it became a soft drink.

2. In England some people eat eggs _____ drink tea for breakfast.

3. Natural spring water is bottled at a spring _____ it is prized for its mineral content.

4. The syrup for colas was first created as a cure for headaches _____ now people drink colas anytime.

5. Carbonated drinks first came only in bottles _____ they later also came in cans.

Name_____

# 130. Reviewing Uses of the Comma

**Insert commas where needed in each sentence.**

1. The European Renaissance started in Italy, and it spread to all the other countries in Europe.

2. The Renaissance, a reawakening of learning, started in about 1350.

3. During the Renaissance scholars rediscovered classical Greek and Roman, and they began to study ancient texts.

4. Painting, sculpture, and architecture began to change at this time too.

5. Three centers of activity were Rome, Florence, and Venice.

6. In Florence, a city in central Italy, the members of the ruling family were patrons of the arts.

7. This family, the Medici, supported many important artists.

8. One of these artists was Michelangelo, a noted painter and sculptor.

9. Michelangelo created beautiful sculptures for the city of Florence, and he created wonderful paintings in Rome.

10. Michelangelo died on February 18, 1564.

11. One person said, "The world has many kings but only one Michelangelo."

12. Other important Renaissance artists are Leonardo Da Vinci, Sandro Botticelli, and Raphael.

13. They painted religious subjects, figures from ancient myths, and portraits of people of the time.

14. Museums around the world show many Renaissance works, and they are appreciated highly today.

15. The Renaissance profoundly influenced art, music, and thought.

16. Bob, do you know where the Renaissance began?

17. Yes, Pam, the Renaissance began in Italy.

18. "The Renaissance," our teacher said, "is one of the most important periods in European history."

19. The *Mona Lisa*, DaVinci's most famous painting, can be seen in the Louvre.

20. You can get information on Italy by writing to the Italian Government Travel Office, 630 Fifth Avenue, New York, New York 10111.

# 131. Using the Semicolon and the Colon

A **semicolon** is used to separate the clauses of a compound sentence when they are not separated by *and*, *but*, *or*, *nor*, or *yet*.

**Until the early 1800s South American was not free; Spain ruled its colonies there with an iron hand.**

A **colon** is used before a list of items.

**Simon Bolivar helped several countries gain their freedom from Spain: Colombia, Venezuela, Ecuador, Peru, and Bolivia.**

A colon is also used after the salutation of a business letter.

**Dear Professor McMurphy:**

**A.** Rewrite the sentences. Replace the coordinating conjunction and the comma with a semicolon.

1. Bolivar was born in South America, and he was the son of an aristocrat.

   [Bolivar was born in South America; he was the son of an aristocrat.]

2. He started his education in Venezuela, but he completed it in Spain.

   [He started his education in Venezuela; he completed it in Spain.]

3. He became interested in politics, and in 1807 he returned to his country to take part in events there.

   [He became interested in politics; in 1807 he returned to his country to take part in events there.]

4. Bolivar became active in politics in 1807, but he was not a leader at first.

   [Bolivar became active in politics in 1807; he was not a leader at first.]

5. Bolivar became president of Colombia in 1819, and later he became president of Peru.

   [Bolivar became president of Colombia in 1821; later he became president of Peru.]

**B.** Insert colons where needed.

1. Three philosophers influenced Bolivar: Locke, Hobbes, and Rousseau.

2. He traveled to several countries: Spain, Italy, England, and the United States.

3. He had several roles in the revolutionary movement: general, president, and political philosopher.

4. Bolivar is a hero in many countries: Colombia, Peru, Chile, Ecuador, Venezuela, and Bolivia.

5. Bolivar did many things: he won battles, he wrote books, and he led countries.

Punctuation & Capitalization

# 132. Using Quotation Marks and Underlining with Titles

**Quotation marks** are used before and after titles of songs, short stories, poems, magazine articles, newspaper articles, and television shows.
Do not use a comma before these titles.

> **The librarian read "The Scarlet Ibis" to the class.**
> **The name of Canada's national anthem is "O Canada!"**

Titles of books, magazines, newspapers, movies, and works of art are usually printed in italics. When these titles are handwritten, they are underlined.

> **Do you read *Newsweek*?**      *Titanic is my favorite movie.*

**A.** Add quotation marks or underlining to the titles.

1. An article about our school was in the <u>Daily News</u> yesterday.

2. The children watched the movie <u>Beauty and the Beast</u> two times!

3. "Secrets of the Bermuda Triangle" airs on public television today.

4. The name of the U.S. national anthem is "The Star-Spangled Banner."

5. I got information for my report from <u>Calliope</u>, a history magazine.

6. The information was in an article titled "Maria Theresa, Empress and Mother."

7. <u>Gone with the Wind</u> is a very famous book and movie.

8. Channel 7 is showing "The Life of Abraham Lincoln" again tonight.

9. We read a beautiful short poem called "Fog."

10. The newspaper had an article called "The Newest Electronic Gadgets."

**B.** Three sentences are punctuated incorrectly. On the line rewrite these sentences using correct punctuation.

1. I just read the book "Treasure Island" by Robert Louis Stevenson.

   [I just read the book <u>Treasure Island</u> by Robert Louis Stevenson.]

2. The <u>New York Times</u> is a very famous newspaper.

   _____

3. We read the short story <u>All Summer in a Day</u> in English class.

   [We read the short story "All Summer in a Day" in English class.]

4. Last week we saw a videotape of the movie <u>Sleeping Beauty</u>.

   _____

5. One of Vincent Van Gogh's most famous paintings is "Starry Night."

   [One of Vincent Van Gogh's most famous paintings is <u>Starry Night</u>.]

# 133. Using the Apostrophe and the Hyphen

An **apostrophe** is used in the following ways: to show possession, with *s* to show the plural of letters, and to show the omission of a letter, letters, or numbers.

> This is Rashid's chair.
>
> I moved here in '99.
>
> Don't misspell Mississippi!
>
> *Mississippi* has two *p*'s, four *i*'s, and four *s*'s, but it has only one *m*.

A **hyphen** is used for the following: to divide a word at the end of a line whenever one or more syllables are carried to the next line; in compound numbers from twenty-one to ninety-nine; and to separate parts of some compound words.

> The best way to understand this problem is to carefully analyze its com-ponent parts and then find a solution.
>
> He graduated from college when he was twenty-one.
>
> My brother-in-law works in England.

**A.** Insert apostrophes where needed.

1. Its Emily Dickinsons poems that I enjoy most.

2. The moons orbit around Earth takes about thirty days.

3. The feeling of patriotism that caused the American Revolution is often called "The Spirit of '76."

4. Theyve just finished reading Longfellows poem "Paul Reveres Ride."

5. We have heard many stories about the blizzard of '01.

6. Ill help you with those boxes, Ms. Jones.

7. The Zócalo is Mexico Citys main plaza.

8. Susan has difficulty writing *r*s and *z*s clearly.

9. Ms. Allan spells her name with two *l*s.

10. She started school in '97.

**B.** Insert hyphens where needed.

1. Niagara Falls is a fast flowing waterfall.

2. Twenty four students went on the field trip to the zoo.

3. A month consists of twenty eight, twenty nine, thirty, or thirty one days.

4. The thyroid is a butterfly shaped gland located in the throat.

5. A black hole is a region in space where gravity is so power ful that not even light can escape it.

Name_____

# 134. Using Capital Letters

**Use capital letters in these places:**

| | |
|---|---|
| THE FIRST WORD IN A SENTENCE | Help is on its way. |
| THE FIRST WORD OF A DIRECT QUOTATION | Patrick Henry said, "Give me liberty or give me death!" |
| PROPER NOUNS AND ADJECTIVES | Let's buy some Colombian coffee. I went to France last year. |
| TITLES OF HONOR BEFORE A NAME | Let's ask Reverend Washington. |
| NORTH, SOUTH, EAST, AND WEST WHEN THEY REFER TO SECTIONS OF THE COUNTRY | The South lost the Civil War. |
| ALL NAMES REFERRING TO DEITIES | The Arabic word for *God* is *Allah*. |
| THE BIBLE OR PARTS OF THE BIBLE, AND OTHER SACRED WORKS | The creation story is in Genesis. |
| THE PRINCIPAL WORDS IN TITLES | Let's watch *Gone with the Wind*. |
| THE PRONOUN *I* | Phil and I walked home together. |
| ABBREVIATIONS WHEN CAPITALS WOULD BE USED IF THE WORDS WERE WRITTEN IN FULL | He is Dr. Ahkook Sawlani, M.D. |
| THE FIRST WORD OF EVERY LINE OF MOST POETRY | Lift ev'ry voice and sing, Till earth and heaven ring . . . |

Use the proofreading symbol (≡) under the letters that should be capitalized.

1. louise remarked, "there is a special message about thanksgiving on the bulletin board."

2. the most important leader of the civil rights movement was dr. martin luther king, jr.

3. petra recited langston hughes's "life is fine" and i recited "harlem."

4. the bible, the koran, and the torah are all important sacred works.

5. fred said, "have you ever been to the smithsonian institution?"

6. *honey, i shrank the kids* is a really funny movie.

7. the name of my dentist is dr. ron oakdale, d.d.s.

8. the robbery case was tried before judge abraham.

9. the west attracted many settlers in the 1800s.

10. pike's peak is in colorado.

# 135. Reviewing Punctuation and Capitalization

**A.** Write the correct punctuation mark in the box.
Then write the name of the punctuation mark on the line.

ACROSS

_____[apostrophe]_____ 1. What☐s the longest river in the world?

_____[exclamation point]_____ 2. Great☐ The Nile is the right answer.

_____[comma]_____ 3. The address of the wildlife organization is
70 E. Falmouth Highway☐ East Falmouth, MA 02536.

_____[colon]_____ 4. There are many endangered species☐ rhinoceroses, pandas,
and tigers.

_____[comma]_____ 5. Anita☐ do you know who wrote *Tom Sawyer*?

_____[apostrophe]_____ 6. It☐s one of Mark Twain's best-loved works.

DOWN

_____[question mark]_____ 1. "Where is Puget Sound☐" asked Nancy.

_____[colon]_____ 2. We studied about Washington state☐ its natural resources,
its history, and its current economy.

_____[commas]_____ 3. We went to the top of the Empire State Building☐ took a
boat to the Statue of Liberty☐ and shopped on Fifth Avenue.

_____[comma]_____ 4. Rockefeller Center is located in New York☐ New York.

**B.** Use the names of the punctuation marks
in Part A to complete the crossword puzzle.

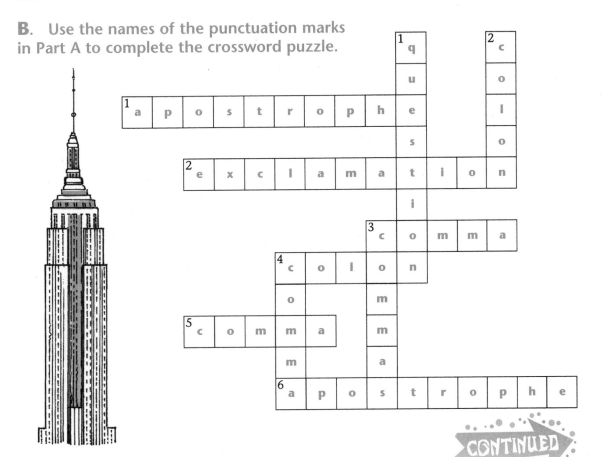

CONTINUED

**C.** Rewrite each sentence with correct punctuation and capitalization.

1. the abbreviation a.l.a. stands for the american library association

   [The abbreviation A.L.A. stands for the American Library Association.]

2. annually the association awards the john newbery medal to an outstanding childrens book

   [Annually the association awards the John Newbery Medal to an outstanding children's book.]

3. no I havent read the latest winner

   [No, I haven't read the latest winner.]

4. in canada the library association there awards a similar prize to a canadian book

   [In Canada the library association there awards a similar prize to a Canadian book.]

5. do you enjoy reading science fiction fantasy or nonfiction

   [Do you enjoy reading science fiction, fantasy, or nonfiction?]

## Try It Yourself

Write four sentences about what you studied in school this week.
Be sure to use punctuation and capitalization correctly.

## Check Your Own Work

Choose a selection from your writing portfolio, your journal, a work in progress, an assignment from another subject, or a letter.
Revise it, applying the skills you have reviewed.
The checklist will help you.

✔ Have you followed the rules for commas?

✔ Have you used quotation marks with direct quotations and around titles of short works?

✔ Have you followed the rules for capitalization?

✔ Do your sentences end with correct punctuation marks?

Name_____

# 136. Identifying Synonyms

> **Synonyms** are words that have the same general meaning.
> You can avoid overworked words such as *nice*, *pretty*, *get*,
> and so forth by using synonyms for these words. You can
> consult a dictionary or a thesaurus to find synonyms.

After each sentence are four words. Circle the letter of the word
that is a synonym for the underlined word.

1. The librarian suggested that Rachel read *Maniac Magee*,
   but she took it out <u>reluctantly</u>.

   a. thoughtfully   b. immediately   (c.) unwillingly   d. carefully

2. Chapter one opens with a <u>disaster</u> involving a high-speed trolley.

   a. struggle   (b.) catastrophe   c. escapade   d. meeting

3. Rachel was afraid that this would be a <u>sad</u> story.

   (a.) pathetic   b. engrossing   c. absorbing   d. strange

4. She was <u>shocked</u> when Jeffrey became a runaway.

   a. accepting   b. mournful   c. frantic   (d.) stunned

5. The laughs begin when the neighborhood becomes <u>interested in</u>
   Maniac Magee's actions.

   a. disturbed by   b. annoyed with   (c.) fascinated with   d. surprised by

6. He was <u>agile</u> as he jumped over fences.

   a. careless   b. fast   (c.) nimble   d. clumsy

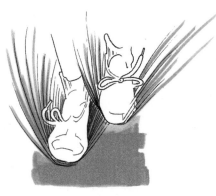

7. His sneakers dissolved into a blur when he
   <u>raced</u> down the field.

   (a.) tore   b. stumbled   c. strolled   d. walked

8. Only Maniac Magee could make living with
   buffaloes a <u>funny</u> experience.

   (a.) humorous   b. alarming   c. happy   d. delightful

9. Jerry Spinelli, the author of *Maniac Magee*, <u>lives in</u> Pennsylvania.

   a. visits   b. endures   c. writes in   (d.) resides in

10. If you haven't read this book, <u>get</u> a copy for yourself!

    a. receive   (b.) obtain   c. prepare   d. persuade

# 137. Working with Synonyms

**A.** In each group of words, cross out the word that does not have the same general meaning as the other three.

| | | | |
|---|---|---|---|
| 1. courteous | polite | ~~magnificent~~ | considerate |
| 2. watchful | ~~indistinct~~ | vigilant | alert |
| 3. remainder | ~~addition~~ | balance | remnant |
| 4. ~~construct~~ | postpone | delay | put off |
| 5. publish | announce | ~~hide~~ | report |
| 6. job | employment | ~~agreement~~ | occupation |
| 7. alike | ~~foremost~~ | identical | same |
| 8. ~~mischievous~~ | pleasant | agreeable | gratifying |
| 9. show | display | exhibit | ~~persist~~ |
| 10. love | adore | ~~annoy~~ | like |

**B.** The overworked words in the following story are underlined. For each of these, substitute a synonym from the list. Write the letter of the synonym you have selected above the overworked words.

| | | | | |
|---|---|---|---|---|
| a. scenic | d. flushed | g. hurriedly | j. reaching | m. shouted |
| b. board | e. grabbed | h. pulled up | k. realized | n. tour of |
| c. depart | f. huge | i. ran | l. removed | o. towering |

"Everybody line up to (1) [b] get on the bus for the field trip," (2) [m] said the principal in a loud voice, as the (3) [f] big yellow school bus arrived. Students ran from all directions and got in line.

Everyone was on the bus, and the bus was getting ready to (4) [c] drive away when Billy's mother (5) [h] drove up with Billy in the car. Billy got out of the car and (6) [i] went over to the bus (7) [g] fast. He looked sleepy. He also looked (8) [d] warm from running to the bus.

Billy sat down and (9) [l] took off his jacket. He sat against the window frame and didn't look at the (10) [a] nice views. He went to sleep.

The rest of us sang songs and looked at all of the (11) [o] tall buildings as we drove downtown. Finally, the bus slowed down. We (12) [k] knew we were (13) [j] coming to our destination. Billy woke up. He (14) [e] took his jacket, and we got ready for our (15) [n] visit to the Natural History Museum.

# 138. Writing an E-Mail

People use e-mail for many purposes. You can use e-mail to extend an invitation. You can use an e-mail to ask for or give information. You can use e-mail to give someone a message.

A good e-mail has a subject line and uses complete sentences.

**A.** Read the example. Circle the subject line.
Leah's e-mail address is ljones@cityschools.org.

| **New Message** | |
|---|---|
| To... | tsmith@cityschools.org |
| Cc... | |
| Subject: | Test tomorrow |

Tanya,

Let's study for tomorrow's social studies test at my house tonight. My mom says that you can stay for dinner too.

Let's start studying right after school. My mom also says she's going to make brownies for us.

Leah

**B.** Write Tanya's response to the e-mail. Tanya wants to study for the test at Leah's house, but she needs a ride home. She needs to ask if Leah's father can give her a ride home at nine o'clock.

| **New Message** | |
|---|---|
| To... | [ljones@cityschools.org] |
| Cc... | |
| Subject: | [Answers will vary.] |

[Answers will vary.]

# 139. Writing a Thank-You Note

A friendly letter has five parts: the date, the greeting, the body, the closing, and the writer's name.

A very common kind of letter is a thank-you note. When you write a thank-you note, it is good practice to start and finish the note with an expression of thanks. It also shows your appreciation to tell how you will use the gift. You might also include some personal news if you like.

**A.** Read the sample letter. The parts are labeled by letter:
(a) date, (b) greeting, (c) body, (d) closing, (e) writer's name.

(a) May 10

(b)  Dear Aunt Phyllis,

   (c) Thank you for the T-shirt you brought me from the San Diego Padres stadium. I love wearing it.

   Did you know that we just got a new dog? Mom says that you need to come over and see her. The dog's name is Samantha, and she is three years old.

   Thanks again for the T-shirt.

(d)  Love,<br>(e)  Tim

**B.** Your grandmother gave you $25 for your birthday. You are going to use the money to buy new clothes for school. Write a thank-you note to your grandmother. Include some family news.   **[Answers will vary.]**

_____ [b]

[e] _____

[c] _____

_____

_____

_____

_____

_____

[a] _____

[d] _____

**C.** Label the parts of your letter. Write letters next to the correct part:
(a) the closing, (b) the date, (c) the body, (d) the writer's name, (e) the greeting.

# 140. Writing a Business Letter

A business letter is more formal than a friendly letter.
It also has more parts. In addition to the (a) date,
(b) greeting, (c) body, (d) closing, and (e) signature,
it also has the address of the (f) sender and the (g) recipient.
In addition, the writer also (h) types his or her name.

**A.** Read the example business letter.

(f)  3440 South Shore Drive
Chicago, IL 60616

(a) May 10, 2001

(g)  Customer Service Department
Music House CDs and Tapes
P.O. Box 141
Atlanta, GA  33412

(b) Dear Customer Service Department:

(c)    Last week I received an order of 4 CDs from you. However,
one of them does not play properly. I am enclosing that CD.
Please send me a new CD that does not skip.

(d) Sincerely,
(e) *William A. Jones*
(h) William A. Jones

CONTINUED

Name_____

**B.** You work in the Customer Service Department of Music House CDs and Tapes. Respond to Mr. Jones. Tell him that you are sorry that the CD was not in good condition. Tell him you are sending a new CD in a separate package. Also tell him that you are enclosing a gift certificate of $5 toward another CD from Music House. Thank him for shopping at Music House.

[c]  [Customer Service Department

Music House CDs and Tapes

P.O. Box 141

Atlanta, GA 33412]

[b]  [Answers will vary.]

[d]  [Mr. William A. Jones

3440 South Shore Drive

Chicago, IL 60616]

[g]  [Dear Mr. Jones:]

[a]  [Answers will vary.]

_____

_____

_____

_____

_____

_____

[e] [Sincerely,]

[f]

[h]

**C.** Label the parts of your letter. Write the letters next to the correct part:
(a) body, (b) date, (c) sender's address, (d) recipient's address, (e) closing,
(f) signature, (g) greeting, (h) sender's name.

# 141. Using the Internet: Evaluating What You Find on the Web

Although the Internet offers a great deal of information, not all of it is credible. Some Internet information may contain errors, or the sources of the information may not be trustworthy. Here are questions to ask yourself as you evaluate information you find on the Internet.

### 1. Is the source of information an expert?

Remember that anyone can post anything on the Internet. A person may know little about a subject, but if the person is clever, the information posted may sound as if it is coming from an expert. Information from government, educational, and most business sites can be trusted. Personal home page Web sites may not be reliable sources on most topics.

### 2. Is the information accurate and true?

Check Internet facts with other sources, such as reference books, magazine and newspaper articles, and adults who know something about your topic. If at least three sources say the same thing, the information is probably correct.

### 3. Is the information up-to-date?

Look for Internet sites that have articles and other items with fairly recent posting dates. Check also to see if there are copyright dates for any of the articles and what those dates are. This is particularly important for topics about science and technology, government, and law.

### 4. Is the information complete?

Are both sides of a topic or issue discussed? If the author gives information that supports only his or her opinion about the topic, important information is probably missing. Politicians or businesses wanting to sell something generally tell only one side of an issue. Look for sites that present both sides.

Think about the four questions on page 151 that you should ask yourself when evaluating Internet information. Next, read each situation below. Then write the number of the question that would be most useful in helping you make sure that you are using reliable information. (You may decide that more than one question would be helpful.)

1. You are writing a research paper about Civil War battles that were fought in your hometown. You find a paper posted on a school Web site about the topic written by a sixth-grader for a social studies class. Would you use this information in your paper?

   [Questions 1 and 2]

2. You read two Internet newspaper articles—one from the *Miami Herald* and one from a supermarket tabloid published in Florida. The articles are about the large number of immigrants who are settling in Florida. Which information source would you use for a report on changing immigration patterns?
   [Questions 1 and 2 to determine which source to use. A student could also make a case for asking Questions 3 and 4 of the final choice.]

3. Your town is considering building a new arts center where plays, musicals, and similar events can be held. One issue is whether the community can afford to build the arts center. An Internet article by a local politician states several reasons why he feels the arts center is too expensive for the town to build. Is this the only information you should use?

   [Question 4. No, sources providing other viewpoints should be consulted.]

4. You are doing research on the causes of global warming. You find a well-written article about this topic posted on the Internet last year. As you scroll to the end of the article, you find that the copyright date of the article is 1995. Is this article a good one to use?

   [Question 3]

# 142. Using Guides to Periodicals

When you do research, you often need to find the latest information about a topic. Guides to periodical literature can be very helpful in finding such information. A **periodical** is anything published at regular intervals of more than one day. Magazines are periodicals; daily newspapers are not.

One helpful guide is the *Children's Magazine Guide.* Articles from about 50 periodicals are indexed in the *Children's Magazine Guide.* It is published monthly from August through March and semimonthly for April and May. August is a yearlong cumulative issue.

All entries are listed in alphabetical order by subject. The *Guide* includes listings for scientific articles, articles about computers, art topics, movie reviews, poetry, and so on. Many subjects are cross-referenced to other subject headings.

Look at the sample entry below, including the labels.

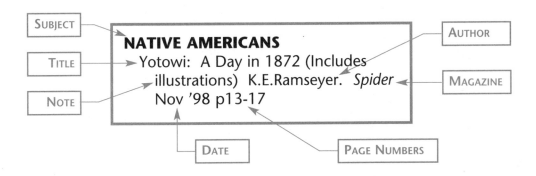

The *Reader's Guide to Periodical Literature* is another index of periodicals. It is published semimonthly and also can be found online in some libraries. In it you can check for information by author or by subject. When you use it, you may need to ask a librarian to help you understand some of the abbreviations.

Name_____

---

**CALIFORNIA CONDOR**
Condors Soar Again. S.Stuckey. *World* Apr '99 p5

**CAMBODIA**
Cambodia. (Includes photographs, illustrations and map) M.Brightman & others. *Calliope* Sep '98 fc-49

**CAMELS**
The Camel Family. (Includes photographs, illustrations and map) J.B.Wexo. *Zoobooks* Mar '99 fc-17
The Girl Who Rode Uncle Sam's Camel. (The Camel Corps; short story) L.Herman. *Hopscotch* Jun-Jul '99 p34-38
My Adventure with Clyde. (Includes photographs) Z.R.Watson. *Highlights* Jul '99 p8-9
Science Corner. *Highlights* Jan '99 p28

**CAMELS - POETRY**
The Camel's Nose. H.Cooper. *Ranger Rick* Sep '98 p44

**CAMOUFLAGE (Animals):** *see* Animal Camouflage

**CAMPING:***see also* Outdoor Cooking; Wilderness Survival
Camping Safety Tips. *Cur Health* Apr-May '99 p20-21

**CANCER - PREVENTION**
Cherry Burgers May Cut Cancer Risk. *Cur Sci* Apr 9 '99 p14

**CANDY:** *see also* Chewing Gum
The Great Halloween Candy Taste Test. *Zillions* Nov-Dec '98 p24-26
Science Never Tasted So Sweet. (Food testers' scientific method) J.D'Agnese. *Sci World* Sep 21 '98 p7-9
Top 5 Holidays for Candy Sales. *Time for Kids* Oct 30 '98 p3

**CANOES AND CANOEING:** *see also* Kayaks and Kayaking; Whitewater Canoeing
Boundary Bounty. (Canoeing in Minnesota; includes photographs) M.Furtman. *Boys' Life* Mar '99 p22-25
Navigating by the Signs of Nature: Canoeing in Micronesia. (Includes photograph and map) C.Sims. *Highlights* Aug '99 p32-33

**CANYONS**
Celebrating Canyon Country. (Grand Staircase-Escalante National Monument; includes photographs and maps) T.H.Watkins. *Nat Geog* Jul '99 p94-109

---

Look at the sample entries above from the *Children's Magazine Guide.* Then answer the following questions.

1. Give one cross-reference for "Canoes and Canoeing."

   **["Kayaks and Kayaking" or "Whitewater Canoeing"]**

2. Who wrote the article about camels entitled "My Adventure with Clyde"?

   **[Z. R. Watson]**

3. In what magazine does the article on Halloween candy appear?

   **[*Zillions*]**

4. What is included as part of the article about Canyon Country by T. H. Watkins?

   **[Photographs and maps]**

5. What is the title of the article about preventing cancer?

   **["Cherry Burgers May Cut Cancer Risk"]**

6. In what month and year did an article about Cambodia appear in *Calliope* magazine?

   **[September 1998]**

7. If you needed information about how animals use camouflage, under what topic heading would you look?

   **[Animal Camouflage]**

8. On what page would you find the article about California condors?

   **[Page 5]**

# 143. Finding Biographical Information

Often in doing research you need to find out information about people—famous and not so well-known but important people. A **biographical dictionary**, which contains basic information about famous people, is one source you could use. This type of reference book may list scientists, politicians, writers, actors, sports figures, and other notable people from long ago to the present day. Some biographical dictionaries may list only women or only African Americans. In book form, such a dictionary is arranged alphabetically by last name.

Each biographical entry lists the following:

- the person's full name

- the person's birth date and, if no longer living, death date

- specific accomplishments of the person and when they occurred—such as records set, books written, and awards won

An online search, by means of a search engine, can also provide biographical information. It may also help you find people closely associated with a particular individual. Note below the entry for Amelia Earhart and related entries found by doing an online search.

---

PERSON'S FULL NAME, LAST NAME FIRST

### The Biographical Dictionary
s9.com/biography

### Result of search for Amelia Earhart

Earhart, Amelia Mary US aviator; as passenger, became 1st woman to fly across Atlantic Ocean 1928; vice-president of Luddington Airlines, Inc. 1930–1931; made 1st female solo trans-Atlantic airplane flight 1932, flying from Newfoundland to Wales; made 1st solo flight from Honolulu to US mainland 1935; made 1st solo flight from Mexico City to New York City 1935; began attempt at around-the-world airplane flight 1937, but disappeared near Howland Island in Pacific Ocean; 2nd wife of George Putnam 1931_1897–1937?

DATE OF DEATH

DATE OF BIRTH

McKneely, Ruckins Jr. (Bo) US aircraft mechanic; tended Amelia Earhart and Fred Noonan's airplane before their ill-fated flight 1937_1908?–1998

Noonan, Frederick J. (Fred) US aviator and navigator; accompanied Amelia Earheart as navigator on attempted around-the-world airplane flight 1937, but disappeared with Earhart near Howland Island in Pacific Ocean_18XX–1937?

SPECIFIC ACCOMPLISHMENTS

Putnam, George Palmer US author, businessman, and publisher; treasurer of G.P. Putnam and Sons 1919–1930; grandson of George Palmer Putnam (1814–1872); husband of Amelia Earhart 1931_1887–1950

---

Use the search results for Amelia Earhart on page 155 to answer the following questions.

1. Why is Ruckins McKneely, Jr., included in the search for Amelia Earhart?

   [Ruckins McNeely, Jr., was the aircraft mechanic who took care of Amelia Earhart and Fred Noonan's plane before it began their attempted around-the-world flight.]

2. There is a question mark after the date of death of both Earhart and Frederick Noonan. Why?

   [Earhart and Noonan have never been found, so no one knows exactly when they died or how.]

3. What was the relationship between Earhart and George Putnam?

   [Amelia Earhart and George Putnam were husband and wife.]

4. What important event occurred in Earhart's life in 1932?

   [In 1932 Amelia Earhart became the first woman to fly solo across the Atlantic Ocean.]

5. Create a time line of Amelia Earhart's life.

   | [1897 | Amelia Earhart is born. |
   | 1928 | Earhart as passenger becomes first woman to fly across the Atlantic Ocean. |
   | 1930-31 | Earhart becomes vice-president of Luddington Airlines, Inc. |
   | 1931 | Earhart marries George Putnam. |
   | 1932 | Earhart flies solo across the Atlantic Ocean. |
   | 1935 | Earhart flies solo from Honolulu to the United States mainland. |
   | | Earhart makes first solo flight from Mexico City to New York City. |
   | 1937 | With Fred Noonan, Earhart begins an around-the-world flight. |
   | | Plane with Earhart and Noonan aboard disappears in the Pacific Ocean near Howland Island.] |

# 144. Finding Books by the Dewey Decimal System

Nonfiction books are arranged on most library shelves in a special way that helps people easily find the topics they are looking for. This system came into use about 125 years ago. It is called the **Dewey Decimal Classification System**, after Melvil Dewey, the man who created it.

All nonfiction books are divided into 10 major subject areas and assigned call numbers. These are the numbers on the spines of library books. The books are put on the shelves in numerical order by their **call numbers**, with books on the same or related topics placed near one another. Here are the 10 major areas and their range of call numbers.

## Dewey Decimal Classification System

| | | |
|---|---|---|
| 000–099 | General Reference | Encyclopedias, almanacs |
| 100–199 | Philosophy and Psychology | Beliefs, morals, personality |
| 200–299 | Religion | Bible, mythology |
| 300–399 | Social Sciences | Education, government, law |
| 400–499 | Languages | Foreign languages, dictionaries |
| 500–599 | Sciences | Astronomy, math, zoology |
| 600–699 | Useful Arts | Business, cooking, medicine, sewing, television |
| 700–799 | Fine Arts | Acting, music, painting, photography, sports |
| 800–899 | Literature | Novels, plays, poetry |
| 900–999 | History | Biography, geography, travel |

Although not shown in the chart above, there also are subdivisions under the major headings. For example, under Fine Arts are subdivisions such as Sculpture (730), Drawing (740), Photography (770), and Music (780).

Some call numbers contain decimals. For example, a book with the call number 770.136 would come before 770.21 on the shelf. Both books would be in the Fine Arts section under the Photography subdivision.

Study the Dewey Decimal Classification System chart on page 157. Then decide under which group of numbers you would look to find books on the following topics.

1. A biographical dictionary ___[000–099 General Reference]___

2. A biography of Jane Goodall ___[900–999 History]___

3. A book of poems for language arts class ___[800–899 Literature]___

4. A collection of Greek myths ___[200–299 Religion]___

5. An almanac for 2002 ___[000–099 General Reference]___

6. Books about African animals ___[500–599 Sciences]___

7. A book about the Inca ___[900–999 History]___

8. A dictionary of Spanish words ___[400–499 Languages]___

9. A book about tornadoes ___[500–599 Sciences]___

10. A travel guide to Germany ___[900–999 History]___

Pick a topic that you might use for a research paper in science or social studies class. Decide which Dewey Decimal System numbers you would look under to find information for your topic. Then go to the library and find and list five books that you might use. Be sure to give both the title and the call number for each book.

[Answers will vary depending on the topics students choose.]

11. _____

12. _____

13. _____

14. _____

15. _____

# Sentence Diagrams

A diagram is a visual outline of a sentence. It shows the essential parts of the sentence *(subject, verb, object, complement)* and the relationship of the other words and constructions to those essentials.

## Diagramming a Simple Sentence

**A.** A simple sentence has one complete thought. This simple sentence has one subject noun, one verb, and one direct object.

**Yesterday many excited children played noisy games in the park.**

Here's how to diagram it.

1. The main line of a diagram is a horizontal line.

   • The verb is written on the center of the diagram line.

   • The subject is written in front of the verb with a vertical line separating it from the verb. This vertical line cuts through the horizontal line.

   • The direct object is written after the verb with a vertical line separating it from the verb. This vertical line touches the horizontal line but does not cut through it.

children | played | games

2. Modifiers of the subject, verb, and direct object are written on slanted lines under the appropriate word. Note the way in which prepositional phrases are indicated

children | played | games
many excited / yesterday in park the / noisy

**B.** These simple sentences have subject complements. Indicate a subject complement by drawing a slanted line pointing back to the subject between the verb and the complement. Remember that the complement can be a noun, a pronoun, or an adjective.

**Mrs. Mitchell is a good teacher. She is always very kind.**

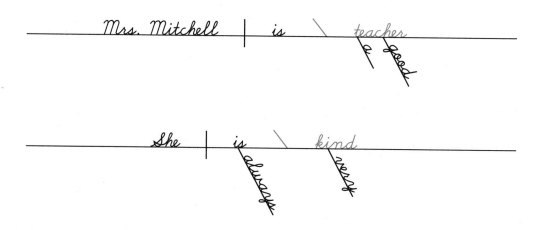

**C.** This simple sentence has a compound subject. Subjects must always appear on horizontal lines. Place the subjects on parallel lines and write the conjunction on a broken line between the words it joins. Add modifiers to the appropriate words.

The tall boy and the short girl won the doubles match.

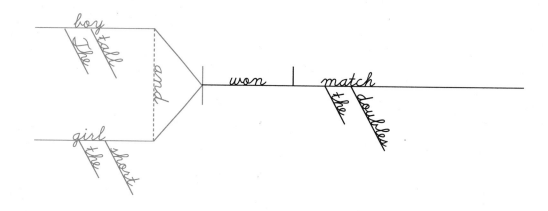

**D.** This simple sentence has a compound predicate. Indicate a compound predicate the same way as a compound subject. Add object, complements, and modifiers to the appropriate words.

The old gardener raked the fallen leaves and mowed the long grass.

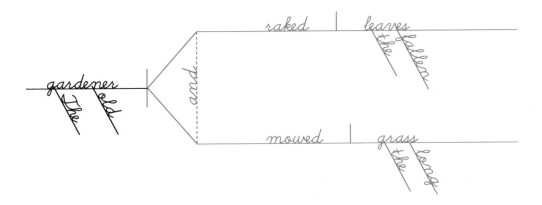

## Diagramming a Compound Sentence

A compound sentence contains two or more independent clauses. Each clause is diagrammed according to the form for a simple sentence. When both independent clauses have been diagrammed, place the conjunction on a horizontal line between the verbs and connect it to the main diagram lines with broken vertical lines.

The longest cave in the world is Mammoth Cave, but the deepest cave is in France.

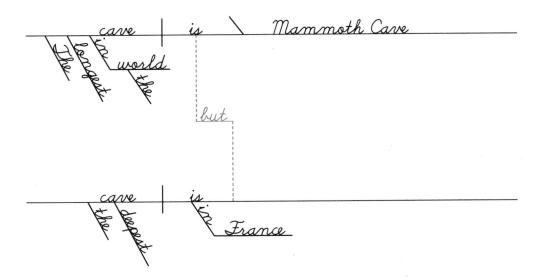

If a semicolon is used instead of a conjunction, place an X on the line between the clauses.

**Snow fell during the night; the field lay under a soft white blanket.**

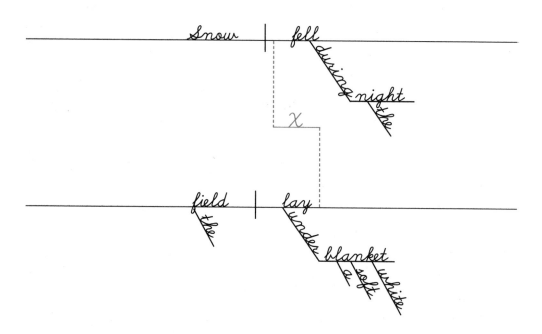

## Try It Yourself

Diagram the following five sentences.

1. A square and a triangle have different characteristics.

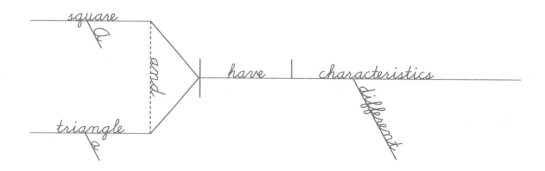

2. Herb and Al designed and built the birdhouse in that tree.

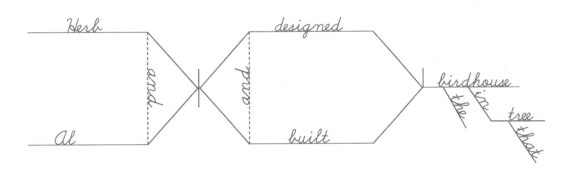

3. The product is the answer in multiplication.

4. Harrisburg is the capital of Pennsylvania, but Philadelphia is the state's largest city.

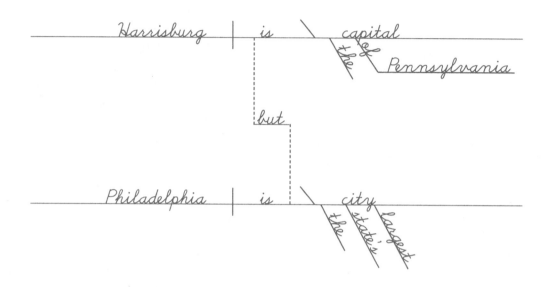

5. Some sharks are huge; others are the size of trout.

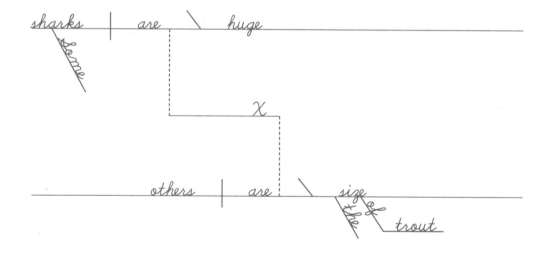

# Handbook of Terms

## A

**adjective** A word that describes a noun or pronoun.

Some descriptive adjectives come from proper nouns and are called proper adjectives. A proper adjective begins with a capital letter: *American* history. Descriptive adjectives that do not come from proper nouns are called common adjectives. A common adjective does not begin with a capital letter: *thick* vegetation.

The adjectives *a, an,* and *the* point out nouns. They are called articles.

Demonstrative adjectives point out specific persons, places, or things.

- *This* and *that* point out one person, place or thing.
- *These* and *those* point out more than one person, place, or thing.
- *This* and *these* point out persons, places, or things that are near.
- *That* and *those* point out persons, places, or things, that are far.

An interrogative adjective is used in asking a question. The interrogative adjectives are *which, what,* and *whose: Which* team has a better record?

Possessive adjectives show possession or ownership. The possessive adjectives are *my, your, his, her, its, our, your,* and *their.*

Numeral adjectives indicate exact numbers: *ten, twenty-five, third, twelfth.*

Some adjectives indicate number but not exact number: *many, few, several, some.*

An adjective usually comes before the noun it modifies: *sunny* morning, *hot* chocolate.

An adjective that follows a linking verb is a subject complement. A subject complement completes the meaning of the verb and describes the subject of the sentence: The night was *dark* and *cold.*

Some words may function as nouns or adjectives: *drama, drama class, property, property tax.*

*See also* **comparison.**

**adverb** A word that modifies a verb, an adjective, or another adverb.

> An adverb of time answers the question *when* or *how often:* It rained *yesterday*. We *usually* eat lunch at noon.

> An adverb of place answers the question *where:* Toshi bent his head *forward*. Sit *here* by the gate.

> An adverb of manner answers the question *how* or *in what manner:* Jason draws *well*. She dances the waltz *gracefully*.

> An adverb of degree answers the question *how much* or *how little*. It may modify verbs, adjectives, or other adverbs. Adverbs of degree include *almost, greatly, merely, quite, too, rather, very, much, hardly, fully, scarcely, barely,* and *partly:* She sings *well*.

> An adverb of affirmation tells that a statement is true. Adverbs of affirmation include *yes, indeed,* and *undoubtedly: Indeed,* he ran the entire marathon.

> A negative idea is expressed by using one negative word, an adverb of negation. This negative word may be *no, not, none, never,* or *nothing*. These words should be used only in sentences that have no other negative words: I do not have *any* (not *no*) apples.

> *See also* **comparison.**

**apostrophe** A punctuation mark (') used in the following ways:

- to show ownership: the *cook's* hat, the *girls'* horses
- to replace letters left out in a contraction: *wasn't* for *was not; I'm* for *I am*
- with *s* to show the plural of letters: Mind your *p's* and *q's*.

**articles** The adjectives *a, an,* and *the. A* and *an* are the indefinite articles. An indefinite article refers to any of a class of things: *a* banana, *an* elephant. *The* is the definite article. The definite article refers to one or more specific things: *the* bananas in the bowl, *the* elephants in the zoo

## C

**capitalization** The use of capital letters. Capital letters are used for many purposes, including the following:

- the first word of a sentence: *The* bell rang.
- an abbreviation if the word it stands for begins with a capital letter: *Rev.* for *Reverend*.
- the first word and the name of a person addressed in the salutation of a letter: *Dear Marie,*

- the first word in the complimentary close of a letter: *Yours truly,*

- the principal words in the titles of books, plays, pictures, and most poems: *A Tale of Two Cities, Romeo and Juliet, Mona Lisa, "Fire and Ice"*

- the first word of a direct quotation: Mother said, " *It's* time for my favorite television program."

- proper nouns and proper adjectives: *China, Chinese* checkers

- titles when used in direct address as substitutes for the names of persons: Thank you, *Professor.*

- North, East, South, West when they refer to a section of the country or the world: the old *West.* They are not capitalized when they refer to direction: He drove *west* on Main Street.

- the pronoun *I,* the interjection *O*

- names referring to deities or to sacred books: *God,* the *Bible*

- two-letter state postal abbreviations: *MA, NY, CA*

**colon** A punctuation mark (:) used after the salutation in a business letter: Dear Sir:

A colon is also used before a list or an enumeration of items: We bought the following: eggs, limes, bread.

**comma** A punctuation mark (,) used to make reading clearer. Among its many uses are the following:

- to separate words or groups of words in a series: elephants, giraffes, hyenas, and monkeys

- to set off parts of dates, addresses, or geographical names: January 1, 2003; 321 Spring Road, Atlanta, Georgia; Paris, France

- to set off words in direct address: Josie, I'm so pleased that you called me this morning.

- after the words *yes* and *no* when they introduce sentences: Yes, I agree with you completely.

- to set off direct quotations, unless a question mark or explanation point is required: "We have only vanilla and chocolate today," he said in an apologetic tone.

- to separate simple sentences connected by the conjunctions *and, but,* and *or:* She called his name, but he didn't answer her.

- after the salutation and closing in a social or friendly letter: Dear Mrs. Porter, Dear Ben, Sincerely yours,

**comparison** The act of comparing. Many adjectives and adverbs can be used to compare two or more persons, places, or things.

Adjectives

- An adjective in the positive degree describes one or more persons, places, or things: The cat is *quiet*. The dogs are *powerful*.
- An adjective in the comparative degree compares two persons, places, or things. Form comparative adjectives by adding *–er* to the positive degree or by putting *more* before the positive degree: *quieter, more powerful*.
- An adjective in the superlative degree compares three or more persons, places, or things. Form superlative adjectives by adding *–est* to the positive degree or by putting *most* before the positive degree: *quietest, most powerful*.

The comparative *fewer* refers to number; the comparative *less* refers to quantity: There are *fewer* apples than oranges. My car uses *less* gas than yours.

Adverbs

- Form the comparative degree by adding *–er* to the positive degree or by putting *more* before the positive degree: *faster, more carefully*.
- Form the superlative degree by adding *–est* to the positive degree or by putting *most* before the positive degree: *faster, most carefully*.

**compound subjects, predicates, objects** In a simple sentence, the subject, the predicate, and the direct object may be compound.

- If a simple sentence has two or more simple subjects, it is said to have a compound subject: *Ivan* and *John* argued with the grocer.
- If a simple sentence has two or more verbs it is said to have a compound predicate: The baby *walks* and *talks* well.
- If a simple sentence has two or more direct objects, it is said to have a compound direct object: Wear your *hat, scarf,* and *gloves*.

**conjunction** A word used to connect words, phrases, or clauses in a sentence. The most common conjunctions are *and, but,* and *or.* Coordinating conjunctions connect subjects, predicates, and direct objects of the same rank and function: Joshua *and* Leanne cut *and* pasted the words *and* pictures on the posters.

Conjunctions connect independent clauses: It poured all day, *and* a cold wind blew. An independent clause has a subject and a predicate and expresses a complete thought.

**contraction** Two words written as one with one or more letters omitted: *doesn't* for *does not, I've* for *I have.*

An apostrophe is used to show the omission of a letter or letters.

Subject pronouns are used with verbs to form contractions: *we're* for *we are, she's* for *she is.*

# D

**dash** A punctuation mark (—) used to indicate a sudden change of thought: The boy jumped—indeed soared—over the hurdle.

**direct object** The receiver of the action of a verb: Nathaniel gave the *baby* to his mother.

An object pronoun can be used as a direct object: Nathaniel gave *him* to his mother.

# E

**exclamation point** A punctuation mark (!) used after an exclamatory sentence and after an exclamatory word or phrase: More than one thousand people attended the wedding! Wonderful! What a celebration!

# H

**hyphen** A punctuation mark (-) used to divide a word at the end of a line whenever one or more syllables are carried to the next line.

The hyphen is also used in the words for compound numbers from twenty-one to ninety-nine and to separate the parts of some compound words: *soldier-statesman, half-baked* plan.

# I

**indefinite pronoun** An indefinite pronoun refers to any or all of a group of persons, places, or things or separately to each member of a group of persons, places, or things. Indefinite pronouns include: *each, either, neither, anyone, no one, anybody, nobody, everyone, everybody, someone, somebody, nothing, something, both, few, many, several, all,* and *some*: Almost *everyone* had a second helping of the pie.

**independent clause** An independent clause has a subject and a verb and can stand on its own as a sentence. Independent clauses are usually connected by the coordinating conjunctions *and, but, or, nor, for,* and *so:* The Cubs play on the north side of Chicago, *and* the Sox play on the south side of Chicago. Independent clauses may also be joined by a semicolon instead of a coordinating conjunction: The Cubs won their series; the Sox lost theirs.

**indirect object** The noun or pronoun that tells to whom or for whom the action in a sentence is done: I gave *him* a present. He cooked *Martha* dinner.

**intensive pronouns** The pronouns ending in *–self* or *–selves (myself, yourself, himself, herself, itself, ourselves, themselves)* can be used to show emphasis: I *myself* cooked the entire dinner.

**interjection** A word that expresses a strong or sudden emotion. An interjection may express delight, disgust, pain, agreement, impatience, surprise, sorrow, wonder, etc. An interjection is grammatically distinct from the rest of the sentence: *Oh! Shh! Ouch! Wow!*

**interrogative pronoun** A pronoun that is used to ask a question.

- *Who* and *whom* are used to ask about persons. *Who* is used when the pronoun is the subject of the sentence. *Whom* is used when the pronoun is the object of a verb or of a preposition.

- *Which* is used to ask about persons, places, or things.

- *What* is used to ask about places or things and to seek information.

- *Whose* is used to ask about possession.

## N

**noun** The name of a person, place, or thing.

There are two main kinds of nouns: common nouns and proper nouns.

- A common noun names any one member of a group of persons, places, or things: *queen, city, church*
- A proper noun names a particular person, place, or thing. A proper noun is capitalized: *Queen Elizabeth, London, Westminster Abbey.*
- A collective noun names a group of persons, places, or things considered as a unit. A collective noun usually takes a singular verb: The *crew* is tired. The *herd* is resting.

- A concrete noun names something that can be seen or touched: *brother, river, tree*. Most nouns are concrete.
- An abstract noun names a quality, a condition, or a state of mind. It names something that cannot be seen or touched: *anger, idea, spirit*.

A noun can be singular or plural.

- A singular noun names one person, place, or thing: *boy, river, berry*.
- A plural noun names more than one person, place, or thing: *boys, rivers, berries*.

The possessive form of a noun expresses possession or ownership. The apostrophe (') is the sign of a possessive noun.

- To form the possessive of a singular noun, add *'s* to the singular form: *architect's*.
- To form the possessive of a plural noun that ends in *s*, add an apostrophe (') to the plural form: *farmers'*.
- To form the possessive of a plural noun that does not end in *s*, add *'s* to the plural form: *children's*.

An appositive is a noun that follows another noun. It renames or describes the noun it follows: Kanisha Taylor, the *president* of our class, will make the first speech.

A noun used in direct address names the person spoken to: *Tyrone*, would you help me?

## O

**order in a sentence** The sequence of the subject and verb in a sentence expresses its order.

- When the verb in a sentence follows the subject, the sentence is in natural order: The *settlers planted* the seeds.
- When the main verb or the helping verb in a sentence comes before the subject, the sentence is in inverted order: Across the plain *marched* the tired *soldiers*.

## P

**period** A punctuation mark (.) used at the end of a declarative or an imperative sentence and after initials and some abbreviations.

**phrase** A group of related words that forms a single unit within a sentence: *beside the sofa; before the storm.*

- An adjectival phrase is used as an adjective and modifies a noun: The book *on the table* is mine.
- An adverbial phrase is used as an adverb and modifies a verb, an adjective, or an adverb: The children played *in the park.*

*See also* **prepositional phrase.**

**possessive adjective** *See* adjective.

**possessive pronoun** A pronoun that shows possession or ownership by the speaker; the person spoken to; or the person, place, or thing spoken about: *mine, yours, his, hers, its, ours, theirs.*

Although possessive pronouns show ownership, they do not contain apostrophes: The new skates are *hers.*

**predicate** The part of a sentence that tells something about the subject. The predicate consists of a verb and its modifiers, objects, and complements, if any: Jason *laughed.* Nikki *ate breakfast.* They *have run through the tall grass.*

**preposition** A preposition is a word that relates a noun or a pronoun to some other word in the sentence. The noun or pronoun that follows the preposition is the object of the preposition: The huge mountain lion leaped *through* (preposition) the tall *grass* (object of the preposition).

Some words may function as prepositions or as adverbs:

- A preposition shows the relationship between its object and some other word in the sentence: Megan sat *near* the door.
- An adverb tells how, when, or where: My friend is always *near.*

**prepositional phrase** A phrase that is introduced by a preposition. A prepositional phrase contains a preposition and an object: *off* (preposition) the *grass* (object of the preposition).

- An adjectival phrase is used as an adjective and modifies a noun: The cabin *in the woods* burned down.
- An adverbial phrase is used as an adverb and modifies a verb: The river flows *into the sea.*

**pronoun** A word that takes the place of a noun or nouns.

A personal pronoun names

- the speaker (first person): *I, mine, me, we, ours, us*
- the person spoken to (second person): *you, yours*

- the person, place, or thing spoken about (third person):
  *he, she, it, his, hers, its, him, her, they, theirs, them*

A personal pronoun is singular when it refers to one person, place, or thing. A personal pronoun is plural when it refers to more than one person, place, or thing.

The third person singular pronoun can be masculine, feminine, or neuter.

A pronoun may be used as the subject of a sentence. The subject pronouns are *I, you, he, she, it, we,* and *they.*

A subject pronoun can replace a noun used as a subject complement.

A pronoun may be used as the direct object of a verb. The object pronouns are *me, you, him, her, it, us,* and *them.*

An object pronoun may be used as the object of a preposition.

*See also* **contraction, possessive pronoun,** *and* **reflexive pronoun.**

# Q

**question mark** A punctuation mark (?) used at the end of a question: What time is it?

**quotation marks** Punctuation marks (" ") used before and after every direct quotation and every part of a divided quotation: "Let's go shopping," said Michiko. "I can go with you," Father said, "after I have eaten lunch."

Quotation marks enclose titles of short stories, poems, magazine articles, television shows, and radio programs. Titles of books, magazines, newspapers, movies, and works of art are usually printed in *italics* or are underlined.

# R

**reflexive pronoun** A reflexive pronoun ends in *-self* or *–selves.* The reflexive pronouns are:

| | |
|---|---|
| myself | ourselves |
| yourself | yourselves |
| himself | themselves |
| herself | |
| itself | |

A reflexive pronoun often refers to the subject of the sentence: She saw *herself* in the mirror.

**semicolon** A punctuation mark (;) used to separate the clauses of a compound sentence when they are not separated by a conjunction: The bicycle was broken; the wheel was damaged.

**sentence** A group of words that expresses a complete thought.

A declarative sentence makes a statement; it is followed by a period: *The sun is shining.*

An interrogative sentence asks a question; it is followed by a question mark: *Where is my pen?*

An imperative sentence gives a command or makes a request; it is followed by a period: *Go to the store. Please pick up the papers.*

An exclamatory sentence expresses strong or sudden emotion; it is followed by an exclamation point: *What a loud noise that was!*

A sentence is made up of a subject and a predicate.

- The subject names a person, a place, or a thing about which a statement is made. The simple subject is a noun or pronoun without any of its modifiers: The *man* is riding his bike.
- The complete subject is the simple subject with all its modifiers: *The tall, athletic young man* is riding his bike.
- The predicate tells something about the subject.
- The simple predicate is a verb without any of its modifiers, objects, and complements: Teresa *waved.*
- The complete predicate is the verb with all its modifiers, objects, and complements: Teresa *waved to the child from the window.*

A simple sentence contains one subject and one predicate. Either or both may be compound.

*See also* **compound subjects, predicates, objects.**

A compound sentence contains two or more independent clauses. An independent clause expresses a complete thought.

- The independent clauses in a compound sentence are usually connected by the conjunctions *and, but, or, nor,* or *yet.*
- A semicolon is used to separate the clauses of a compound sentence when there is no conjunction.

*See also* **order in a sentence.**

**subject** The person, place, or thing that a sentence is about: *Daniel* spoke. The *prairie* was dry. The *cup* broke into pieces.

**subject complement** A word that completes the meaning of a linking verb in a sentence. A subject complement may be a noun, a pronoun, or an adjective: Broccoli is a green *vegetable*. The prettiest one was *she*. The sea will be *cold*.

**synonym** Synonyms are words that have the same general meaning: *big* and *large*.

# V

**verb** A word that expresses action or state of being.

A verb has four principal parts: the present, the present participle, the past, and the past participle.

- The present participle is formed by adding *–ing* to the present.
- The simple past and past participle of regular verbs are formed by adding *–ed* or *–d* to the present.
- The simple past and past participle of irregular verbs are not formed by adding *–ed* or *–d* to the present.

The tense of a verb shows the time of its action.

- The simple present tense tells about an action that happens again and again: I *play* the piano every afternoon.
- The simple past tense tells about an action that happened in the past: I *played* the piano yesterday afternoon.
- The future tense tells about an action that will happen in the future; the future is formed with the present and the auxiliary verb *will:* I *will* play in the piano recital next Sunday.
- The present progressive tense tells what is happening now; the present progressive tense is formed with the present participle and a form of the verb *be:* He *is eating* his lunch now.
- The past progressive tense tells what was happening in the past; the past progressive tense is formed with the past participle and a past form of the verb *be:* He *was eating* his lunch when I saw him.
- The present perfect tense tells about a past action that is relevant to the present: She *has gone* to this school for two years.
- The past perfect tense tells about a past action that happened before another action in the past. She *had gone* to Banks School before she moved to Boston.

*(continued on next page)*

A transitive verb expresses an action that passes from a doer to a receiver. The receiver is the direct object of the verb: The dog *ate* the bone.

An intransitive verb has no receiver of the action. It does not have a direct object: The sun *shone* on the lake.

Some verbs may be transitive or intransitive according to their use in the sentence: Chita *played* the harp. Joel *played* at Notre Dame.

A linking verb links a subject with a subject complement (a noun, a pronoun, or an adjective).

- The verb *be* in its many forms *(is, are, was, will be, have been,* etc.) is the most common linking verb.
- The verbs *appear, become, continue, feel, grow, look, remain, seem, smell, sound, stay,* and *taste* are also considered to be linking verbs.

A verb phrase is a group of words that does the work of a single verb. A verb phrase contains one or more auxiliary or helping verbs *(is, are, has, have, will, can, could, would, should,* etc.) and a main verb: She *had forgotten* her hat.

A subject and a verb must always agree.

- Singular nouns and singular subject pronouns must have singular verbs. The third person singular of the simple present tense ends in –*s* or –*es*: I *run*. You *run*. He *runs*.
- Plural nouns and plural subject pronouns must have plural verbs. A plural verb does not end in –*s* or –*es*: We *run*. You *run*. They *run*.
- Use *am* with the first person singular subject pronoun: I *am* a soccer player.
- Use *is* with a singular noun or a third person singular subject pronoun: Paris *is* a city. She *is* a pianist. It *is* a truck.
- Use *are* with a plural noun, the second person subject pronoun, or a third person plural pronoun: Dogs *are* good pets. You *are* the winner. We *are* happy. They *are* my neighbors.
- Use *was* with a singular noun or a first or third person singular subject pronoun: The boy *was* sad. I *was* lucky. It *was* a hard job.
- Use *were* with a plural noun, a second person subject pronoun, or a third person plural subject pronoun: The babies *were* crying. You *were* a good friend.
- Use *doesn't* with a singular noun or a singular subject pronoun: He *doesn't* have a pencil. The teacher *doesn't* have a pen.

- Use *don't* with a plural noun, a second person subject pronoun, or a third person subject pronoun: Buses *don't* stop here. You *don't* have the tickets. We *don't* have to go.

In sentences beginning with *there,* use *there is* or *there was* when the subject that follows is singular: *There is* no cause for alarm. Use *there are* or *there were* when the subject is plural: *There were* many passengers on the bus.